MONASTIC WISDOM SERI]

Matthew Kelty, ocso

Singing for the Kingdom

The Last of the Homilies

MONASTIC WISDOM SERIES

Patrick Hart, ocso, General Editor

Advisory Board

Michael Casey, ocso   Terrence Kardong, osb
Lawrence S. Cunningham   Kathleen Norris
Bonnie Thurston   Miriam Pollard, ocso

MONASTIC WISDOM SERIES: NUMBER FIFTEEN

Singing for the Kingdom

The Last of the Homilies

by

Matthew Kelty, ocso

Edited with an Introduction by
William O. Paulsell

CISTERCIAN PUBLICATIONS
Kalamazoo, Michigan

Cistercian Publications, 2008
All rights reserved

Cistercian Publications
Editorial Offices
The Institute of Cistercian Studies
Western Michigan University
Kalamazoo, Michigan 49008-5415
cistpub@wmich.edu

*The work of Cistercian Publications is made possible in part by support from
Western Michigan University to The Institute of Cistercian Studies.*

Library of Congress Cataloging-in-Publication Data

Kelty, Matthew.
Singing for the kingdom : the last of the homilies / Matthew
Kelty ; edited with an introduction by William O. Paulsell.
p.   cm. (Monastic wisdom series ; no. 15)
ISBN 978-0-87907-015-1
1. Catholic Church—Sermons.   2. Sermons, American—
20th century.   I. Paulsell, William O.   II. Title   III. Series.

BX1756.K418S56   2008
252'.02—dc22

2008003587

Printed in the United States of America

CONTENTS

INTRODUCTION

While living in a small, experimental monastery in eastern North Carolina, Matthew Kelty was invited to speak to the students at a nearby Protestant college. After his talk, a member of the English Department faculty described him as a poet, a dancer, and a singer. That may well be the most accurate description of Matthew, as these homilies will attest.

Matthew Kelty was born in 1915 in the Boston area. His real name was Charles, but when one becomes a monk one is given a new name to indicate a new life. While attending public schools he discovered that there were such things as monasteries, but he didn't know they still existed.

Wanting to serve God and the Church, he joined a missionary order, the Divine Word Society (SVD), was trained, ordained, and sent to New Guinea. The loneliness of his time in New Guinea was painful, and eventually he was brought home to edit the promotional magazine of the order, *The Christian Family*. The magazine closed down after ten years and Matthew looked for a new direction for his life.

He was attracted to the Abbey of Gethsemani in Kentucky and was admitted in 1960. He often said, "Getting up in the middle of the night, putting on nice clothes, and singing psalms; that's the life for me." The monks, he said, witness to the Kingdom of God by singing. He was trained as a novice by Thomas Merton whom he described as "tough."

He served in various capacities at the monastery, eventually becoming the chaplain in the retreat house. After the final service of the day, the office of Compline, he would give talks to the retreatants in the Guest House chapel. The talks were well attended and much loved by people. Those who made retreats year after year would often hear the same talks several times, but they didn't mind. They enjoyed Matthew's energy, style, and sense of humor. He would always begin by reading half a dozen poems, often explaining their context, giving a word about the poet, and saying why he liked the poem. Most were well known to the listeners. Occasionally, he would say that he didn't really understand a particular piece. One evening he read a poem by Thomas Merton he couldn't quite figure out. "It's vigorous, you have to give him that," he said.

In 2005 an illness made it impossible for him to continue as chaplain, much to the disappointment of the retreatants. In November of that year he celebrated his 90th birthday. He moved to the monastery infirmary but continues to attend the monastic liturgy and occasionally deliver homilies to the monks. This volume is the fourth collection of these talks, delivered to the monks on various occasions. They reveal much about the monastic life, especially those in the first section.

Before becoming chaplain he had a series of other adventures. On June 24, 1970, the feast day of John the Baptist, he moved to Oxford, North Carolina, to lead a small monastery that Gethsemani had acquired. The idea was that half a dozen monks would reside there in simple surroundings, living contemplative lives but free from maintaining a large abbey. They supported themselves by weaving. There were never more than three or four monks there, and, for a time, Matthew was the only resident. Still, retreatants found their way there and learned from him.

On one occasion he walked from Oxford to Washington, D.C., to protest the Vietnam War. He had a conflict with the local bishop for having the telephone removed from the monastery. He did not want to pay the federal phone tax that supported the war.

Although the Oxford community was small and isolated, he had a growing desire to live a more solitary life. In June, 1973, he returned to Gethsemani where he went through a ceremony of marriage to Lady Solitude. On the feast day of John the Baptist of that year he left for Papua New Guinea where he would live as a hermit for nine and a half years. Eventually, Gethsemani called him back, deciding that at his age it would be wise for him to live in community. Thus began his chaplaincy.

These homilies reveal many things about Matthew. He complains about the community's resistance to new ideas but understands the way monasteries work. He describes the remodeling of the monastery church and his love for the new version. The values that are important to him are those seen in opera, ballet, sculpture, painting, song and dance, poetry, daffodils and hyacinths. The dearest thing to him, he said, was the Latin Divine Office. For him, monastic liturgy was song and dance.

In a little booklet he produced for prospective monks, *Aspects of the Monastic Calling*, he wrote, "We like it if you can listen to music and play some. We like it if you notice rain, feel the wind, hear the birds, smell the soup. We like you to be aware, not asleep; alive, not dead; in touch, not gone." When a college student asked him why he became a monk, Matthew replied, "Somebody has to walk in the rain!"

He loved the Mass, calling it the greatest of the sacraments. He was sad that non-Catholics did not enjoy the riches of Marian devotion. He once asked the monks, "How many of you found here what you expected?" He certainly had no idea what was ahead of him when he entered the life. What motivated the men to become monks? Matthew guessed that it was a love of quiet, for only in quiet can one ponder the mysteries of God and the ultimate questions. In his talks to retreatants he often asked, "Where did we come from, why are we here, where are we going?" He has an absolute faith in immortality, to answer the last one. It shows up in many of these homilies.

A group of Protestant divinity school students visited Gethsemani in 1958, before Matthew's arrival. One of the students asked a monk, "What is the purpose of this life?" The monk replied, "To witness to the transcendence of God." Matthew says the same in the third piece in this collection.

The monastic life is not without its moments of good humor. Matthew tells of driving a borrowed red convertible to the monastery Post Office, scandalizing a group of visitors who thought he ought to be in the cloister. He was clearly enjoying himself. We are told about a monk who wanted to plant some seeds, but the abbot refused to let him buy them because the price had gone up from ten to twenty-five cents. When the monk complained to his friends, they sent him more packets of seeds than he could possibly plant which, Matthew said, everyone knew would happen anyway.

He was certainly aware of what was going on in the world. There is mention in these homilies of priestly immorality. He expresses his opposition to capital punishment. He knows the church is not perfect and is aware that everyone wrestles with evil.

He wrote his autobiography, *Flute Solo,* as well as articles and a handbook for those considering the monastic life. He never considered himself to be in the same intellectual class as Thomas Merton, yet he is clearly well read, well informed, and, as retreatants discovered, able to converse intelligently on a wide variety of subjects. His humility masks a deep and creative thinker.

These homilies communicate the beauty and the joy of the monastic life. For those who have doubts about the faith, about monasticism, about their own destinies, Matthew provides much guidance and food for thought.

These homilies were delivered over a period of five years, generally 2000–2005. Often they are related to the themes of the liturgical year. The gospel readings for the day are usually indicated, although Matthew sometimes did not refer to them. However, it would be a good idea to read the passages and then see the unique meaning Matthew gives to them when he does address them.

Matthew mentions that it takes many people to produce one poet or one artist or one singer. It, no doubt, took many people to produce a Matthew Kelty: the Boston public schools, the Divine Word Society, the natives of New Guinea, the people of eastern North Carolina, hundreds of retreatants, and the monks of Gethsemani. This volume celebrates a remarkable life of creativity, service, and faith.

During his years as a hermit in New Guinea he wrote letters to friends. One of those letters contained these words: "Everyone, no matter what his state, needs some time alone, some hours of peace, of quiet; time to ponder and dwell with things, to let things be. For once we put our tools down and close our mouths and turn the lights out and the music off, and listen: to the wind, if you will. To the birds. To your own breathing. To the God hidden in the quiet of your own abandoned heart."

That, for Matthew Kelty, is the monastic life.

Father Matthew reached the age of 91 in 2006. Feeling that he had fulfilled his ministry as a community homilist, he asked the Abbot to be relieved of that duty. So, these are the last of his homilies.

ACKNOWLEDGEMENTS

A word of thanksgiving is in order to Brother Chrysostom Castel, who transcribed these homilies as Father Matthew Kelty had handwritten them, which was not always legible. He was also responsible for having them made available on the World Wide Web during these last years when Kelty was ministering to the Gethsemani Community in this way.

THE MONASTIC LIFE

SEEKING AUTHENTIC REALITY

Luke 3:10-18

When our Abbot General, Dom Gabriel Sortais, came here for a Visitation, he talked about a little holy card someone had given him. It was a picture of a clown in his dressing room putting on paint before the mirror as he gets ready for his act. He says, smiling, "Who doesn't put on a little paint?" "*Qui se ne grise pas un peu?*"

William Shickel was here on retreat recently. He is from Loveland, Ohio, and was the designer for the church complex over thirty years ago. His visit brought back memories.

The choir monks and juniors and novices spent most of the 1960s redoing the monastery. The Brothers carried on their regular work. It was hard, noisy, dirty manual labor, but we ended up with a handsome scriptorium, chapter room, and refectory, not to mention the rooms of the monks and other areas. Since the church was next, Brother Clement and Brother Giles suggested to Dom James, our abbot, that perhaps it would be wise to hire a designer and have it all done commercially. Otherwise it would take too long. Since monks meddled effectively in such projects, they would be sure the final product was worthy.

On the advice of the editor of *Liturgical Arts Magazine* they hired Shickel for his answer to their one query, "What do you think of Shaker art?" He said it was his basic inspiration. "Then you're our man. We want something simple, honest, and authentic."

When he saw the church, Shickel knew he had a gem. But the gem was covered with lath and plaster to make it something it wasn't. So he gathered a host of photos of Cistercian abbey churches in Europe and told the monks, "You can have something like that if you remove the plaster. A beautiful woman doesn't need paint."

It took a lot of discussion, but the monks agreed. Shickel got a gold medal from the Cincinnati chapter of the American Institute of Architects and another from the Ohio state chapter for his work. It was not that they were into Cistercian architecture; they knew a good thing when they saw it. Shickel didn't create it. It was already there. Only the steeple didn't fit and it was coming down anyway. Dom James had already built a new one.

At least some of you know who Robert Mitchum, the actor, is. He of the droopy eyelids. Many years ago he was arrested for smoking marijuana and given ninety days. The reporters were waiting for him when he emerged. "How was it, Mr. Mitchum?" "Just like Beverly Hills," he said. "Without the riff-raff." That sounds like a wisecrack, but it was an astute observation. If prisons and prisoners are anything, it is that both are brutally honest. Politician, doctor, plumber, lawyer, sailor, addict, even priest, you may have been. Here you're just a public sinner, a felon, a crook. Here is no camouflage.

Prisons are like monasteries, but not for having walls and poverty and celibacy, obedience, a common table, and work and cells, even solitude, but because they are cruelly honest. Human frailty is exposed. But alas, there is no healing love, no love of Christ, of one another in a prison. It is love that makes the monastery, not the structure.

The monastic life is honest. In Beverly Hills one hides in wealth, in pleasure, in power, in coming and going, clothes and parties. One's career and one's fame hide the reality beneath. Sinners all and no one adverts to that. Paint hides all that. Actors all, surrounded by stage scenery, remote from reality.

All are sinners, and to admit it is to submit ourselves to healing love and respond to that love in Christ and one another in the fact of utter reality.

This is not to say a Cistercian style is a must, that there is no other way. No. We had our turn. A new generation has theirs. But you ought to know where we are coming from. The utter sincerity of our buildings—genuine, authentic, and real—helps us cultivate the same with ourselves and with one another. We need not pretend we are other than we are, and we can do that in the power of grace, God's love for us.

So, the answer to the question, "Who doesn't put on a little paint?" We don't. That's why we saw no need to make a Cistercian church look Gothic, even poor man's Gothic, American Gothic in plaster and lath.

Father Louis (Thomas Merton) complimented Shickel on what he had done: "I just want to tell you what a splendid job I think you did in our abbey church. I particularly like the interior of the church: bright, simple, clean-cut, no nonsense, and perfectly in accord with the spirit of our life."

Now with Advent, a new year, we are off yet again for the authentic; not in mere architecture, but in the architecture of the spirit, authentic Christians, authentic monks, in an authentic monastery. We try again or die in the attempt. Amen.

SUPPLE LOVE

Mark 2:1-12

For the past ten years or so I have been offering Mass each day after Vigils in the chapel with the Roman Canon and sung according to the music printed at the rear of the Missal. You would think, wouldn't you, that others might take up the practice, not of a daily Roman Canon or after Vigils, but sung? Granted that we do not have an abundance of priests, some of them can sing at least as well as I do. No takers. Why? One could take it personally and say, "Well, no one takes up any ideas I suggest." But that would be silly. And incorrect. It's more a generic thing, characteristic of monastic communities, especially religious communities. They tend to be conservative, are traditionally oriented, don't relish change, least of all being trendy.

When Brother Roger was last here, he told me that he was working for a while for his brother, a sign maker.

"Ah," I said. "That's great. I wonder if he works with neon."

"Yes, he works with neon."

"Fine. I have an idea. I'd like a large cross in blue neon on the water tower on the hill. You know, it looks like a mighty Easter candle. We could Easter-candle it and mount a long strip of blue up and down, and a strip across for a cross. And the year 2000 at the center. Maybe an Alpha and Omega at the end of the cross arms. Could he do that?"

"Sure, he could do that. No problem."

"For the millennium, you know. So people going by wouldn't think the place is some school or prison. How much do you think?"

"Oh, a couple of thousand."

So, I submitted it to the council. It didn't even make the minutes. So, it's personal? They don't take up any suggestion I offer? No, not at all. It's generic. They don't cotton to new ideas. They resist innovations. It's characteristic.

Christ's encounter this morning at Capernaum is revealing. A group had gathered in the house where he was staying. He was giving them the good news he came to proclaim when they brought a young paralytic to Him, hoping He would heal him. But they couldn't get close enough to ask Him. So they climbed up on the roof, removed the tiles and lowered the paralytic to a place close to his feet. Christ would have been somewhat amazed, or more likely amused, at their determination. He looked with affection on the youth and told him to "be of good heart, for I forgive your sins."

The scribes prominent in the gathering reacted in character, distressed at the unheard of presumption. They raised their eyebrows, gave each other knowing looks. They pursed their lips and nodded knowingly. Christ need not have read their minds. He had only to look at their faces.

"The man blasphemes! Who can forgive sin but God alone?"

Their general reaction blinded them to the obvious. If only God can forgive, maybe He is God.

"Which is easier, to heal or forgive?"

"Get up and go home," he said to the youth. High drama in a low room packed with a delighted audience who rubbed it into the traditionalists. "We have never seen anything like this, have we now?"

We are going to elect a new abbot for this house in a month or two. It surely cannot be out of place to suggest that some concern over our generic tendency to stick to what we are used to will need some deft handling.

Hopefully, we shall elect a new abbot even better than the one we had. We stiffen that hope with prayer. That hope being somewhat unrealistic, we pray that at least we get one as good as what we've had.

Yet, one thing is certain. Whether he is better than what we had or as good or far worse, he will assuredly be different. His being different will require some openness, some give in your stance, some limber in your muscle if you are going to survive. Your commitment is going to have to go deeper than merely being comfortably content with what you are used to, to a deep submission to God's will revealed in his providence.

Which, after all, is an application of our faith common to all. Conformity to God's will is the key to happiness. Any generic inertia that resists change can lead us far astray, as it led the scribes astray. That we must avoid at any cost. Better then to bend than to break, better keep flowing rather than freeze. No sky-scraper ever broke in the wind. They bend. No vowed life ever lasted without supple love. Amen.

WITNESSES TO THE TRANSCENDENT

Luke 1:57-66, 80

I was in my hermitage in Bogia on the north coast of Papua New Guinea only a week or so when the local government man came by to see what I was up to. He was a young nominal Catholic from Australia. He took a look around. "So you're a hermit?" he said.

"In a manner of speaking, yes, I am."

"Well, I've seen some real hermits. I visited Greece and saw some. They lived in caves on the mountainside and got their supplies by a rope lowered to someone below the cliff."

My layout, by comparison, seemed rather remote from anything like that. "Yes," I said, "I've read of them. A monk I know visited them and told me about them."

He was not impressed by my remarks, nor by me, nor by my scene. He invited me to come down the next day and have a beer. His companion snickered.

So, the next day, out of courtesy, I went down and had a beer with him. As we were talking his cook walked past the cooler and came back with an enormous raw steak on a platter. "Man," I thought, "he's really going to rub it in." But happily he did not invite me to lunch. The steak was for him. So at least I was spared his bragging about the hermit he had down for steak and a beer.

Our relationship with John the Baptist is somewhat similar. We are far removed from a life similar to that of John the Baptist. Yet he has been and continues to be a favorite of monks. In fact, I made my vows thirty-nine years ago on this day. And my hermit vow some years later. And my original vows sixty years ago at the same time.

What, then, is the connection? St. John lived a lifetime in the desert in a kind of ascetic solitude we only dream of. He became a great preacher when the time came, announcing the coming of the Kingdom and of the Messiah, warning all to repent and to be converted. Nor was this message gentle and restrained. It was the opposite: strong, forthright, fearless. His condemnation of the loose living of Herod led to his violent death. As a model for monks he seems rather too much of a good thing.

So, the attraction for him lies more than in a commendation of a lifestyle. Rather, it was what he was in the total picture, which means to say he was a witness by his life and his death. It is in being a witness that we are his disciples. We are what we preach. Or, rather, our preaching is our being.

We are witnesses to the transcendent. If all Christians are that, monks would be so in a more articulate way, even a dramatic way. Our life makes no sense except spiritually. We bear witness to the transcendent. It was never meant to be practical, not even in the sense of pastoral service of some kind.

In concrete terms, who needs fruitcake? Or fudge? Or cheese? That is not where we are. That is not what we are here for.

We are not mendicants, a valid form of witness. We are monks. We earn our own living. That is but a part of the whole picture: a community of celibate monks, following a rule of life, under an abbot. The rule of life involves a regimen of common prayer, of community, of service, of study and reading, under obedience, in a life of shared goods, committed to the love of God and one another in peace and mercy. It is—to say the least that can be said—a beautiful life. It is a significant witness to a very deep level. It is a great work of God.

One might call it an art form, if that appeals to you. Like any art, not particularly practical. Who needs ballet?

Yet art is of enormous significance to the human scene, even if that significance cannot be measured in practical terms. Song and dance, painting and sculpture, symphony and poetry, beauty in any form is an elemental aspect of the human scene. Without them, life becomes utterly dreary.

But we are a world away from the typical art form because this art form is a living reality. It is people who are this art form. The art form is not only living people, but a living people immersed in the life and love of God. This art form is alive, both humanly and divinely. It is therefore unique.

As in the mysteries of faith, we do not merely read about them, study them, reflect on them. We do them. The Passion, Death, and Rising of Christ are not merely recalled and celebrated. They continue through history, and we participate in that continuation. Christ lives and dies and rises among us. His life and grace permeate the whole of us. Here is art of another sort. Here is a witness of staggering beauty and significance. It is God in the human scene in a most specific way.

To be called to such a witness is a great grace, a remarkable gift. This past week we bore witness to one such life coming to fruition in death, and another making a solemn commitment to it. And old monk and a young one.

What a gift to the world! An art of any kind is a grace to the human scene. Here is an art that is vivid with grace. Here is God in the human scene made evident and obvious.

This witness is as valid as John's was, and as powerful. The witness may be as remote from the style of John's witness as one can be, yet the witness is one of a kind. That's why he means so much to us. We understand him and what he is. The meaning of his life is clear to us. We are in the same category or, if you like, the same art form.

Monks, too, die as tragically as John did. Every nation has at one time or another turned on the Church. A prime victim is the monastery. If there are monasteries all over Europe, there are monastic ruins too that are still haunting memories of extraordinary beauty.

So, carry on in great joy and great gratitude. We are a blessed group to be called to such a remarkable witness. God grace our efforts to make this home one of special beauty, the living God revealed. Having a beer once in a while does not spoil it, as the government man thought it did. Amen.

WE SING FOR THE KINGDOM

Luke 23:35-43

We do not end the liturgical year with a whimper, that is sure. We end, rather, on a note of triumph. We are bold and talk of kings and kingdoms, realms and all that.

Though Christ Himself declared it, "Yes, I am king," when Pilate asked Him, it was only in 1925 with Pius XI that we got around to making something of it in a feast day.

The trumpets blare in St. Peter's: "Christus vincit, Christus regnat, Christus imperat." Christ conquers, Christ rules, Christ reigns. He does indeed.

It says so in the Preface of the Mass of the day:

> As King he claims dominion over all creation that he may present
> to you his Almighty Father an eternal and everlasting Kingdom:
> a Kingdom of truth and life,
> a Kingdom of holiness and grace,
> a Kingdom of justice, love, and peace.

Beautiful. Unquestionably beautiful. But, where is it? Good question.

Jesus answered that and said, "It is among you, within you. It is here now." And we would say, "We are working on it, with you. It is here now. We promise you."

And that's true, of course. It is here. It is on the way. It is coming.

And we expedite the coming. Are involved in it. How? Obviously, by music. By chant. By song.

I call your attention to it. If it borders on the absurd to make cheese and fruitcake and fudge for the Kingdom, and we do, I call your attention to worse than that:

We sing for it.

This is a house of music, of song. Seven times a day we gather to sing songs.

To God. To Christ. For us and for the world.

I beg you, enter into the poetry of this beautiful truth.

We sing for the coming of the Kingdom. It is perhaps the most significant contribution we could make.

What else surpasses it in beauty and meaning?

Seven times a day we gather to sing to God for the world. How practical! How down to earth! We have been doing it since we got here on December 21, 1848. The song began the next day, December 22, and has never ceased. Praise God!

Note how beautiful the song:

> A thousand years old—much of the chant.
> Quality music: the human voice, in many modes, in haunt-ing melodies, day by day, week by week, year by year, on and on until the end.

We live in a house of music. If a world around us is de-stroyed by an unending output of rubbish, we are immersed in a climate of music, in a house resonant with music, which is at once superbly pure, elegant, involving the whole person and the whole community one way or other. But it is also healing for us and for all the world.

It is at once communal and anonymous, in unison and highly personal. This music is of the head, of the heart, and of the gut. It is of the head because it is based on scripture and the events of God's life. It is of the heart because love is involved. Love is the gist of it, love for Christ, love for one another, love for the world. It is of the gut because emotionally this music is powerful, but in a deep, deep way, far beyond the mere noise and din of the world. It is chaste music, discreet and benign.

We live in a house of music, of song. All are affected by it, be they directly involved or not. All in some way achieve it, make it possible. All share in it for the world, each a center of peace, the whole a presence of peace.

Chant has power and heals. You cannot sing to God day after day and still be governed by anger, resentment, fury, frustration or contempt. You cannot continue. You submit to healing and accept it. Hence, a chant is healing, and a house of chant is healing, for us and for the world.

So, we build the Kingdom. It is coming, and we hasten its coming. We expedite it.

An expert on chant claims that a major aspect of the development of a Christian culture in medieval Europe was chant. The mere sound of it was productive. It permeated society.

In a wild, noisy, violent world, we sing. We sing old songs, rich in history, rooted in it, graced by God, for healing, ours and the world's. This is the heart of Gethsemani, its point, purpose, and meaning for the building of the Kingdom. Amen.

A BONDING BEAUTEOUS

John 2:1-11

We lived across the street from St. Agatha's church in Milton, Massachusetts, when I was a boy. Over time we noticed that little old ladies used to come to watch weddings. They would sit in the back or on the side and enjoy it all no end. Presumably they were happily married, else they would not likely seek to revive old and sweet memories in seeing young love of today set out on a life together.

Christ's first public sign was at the wedding in Cana when, at the suggestion of his Mother, and his Father's concurring will, he supplied wine for want of enough for more guests than were anticipated. The significance of the episode does not escape us.

The three espousals of Christ are at work here: his marriage to Israel as his bride; his marriage to the Church, the new Israel; and his marriage to every Christian soul in a union of love.

As God says through the prophet Hosea, speaking of Israel, "So I will allure her. I will lead her into the desert and speak to her heart. I will espouse you to me forever. I will espouse you in right and in justice, in love and in mercy. And you shall know the Lord" (Hosea 2:14, 19-20).

In Vatican II's *Lumen Gentium* we read:

> The Church, "that new Jerusalem which is above," is also called "our Mother" (Galatians 4:26). She is described as the spotless spouse of the spotless Lamb (Apocalypse 19:7). She it was whom Christ "loved and delivered himself up for her that he might sanctify her" (Ephesians 5:26), whom he unites to himself by an unbreakable covenant, and whom he unceasingly "nourishes and cherishes" (Ephesians 5:29). Once she had been purified, he willed her to be joined unto

himself and to be subject to him in love and fidelity (Ephesians 5:24). Finally, he filled her with heavenly gifts for all
eternity, in order that we might know the love of God and
of Christ for us, a love which surpasses all knowledge.
(Ephesians 3:19)

What applied to Israel and the Church also applies to the
individual. Baptism involves a marriage bonding with Christ.
The Song of Songs in the Bible has been understood as describing
the spiritual union of Christ and the church and Christ and the
individual. Marriage, according to one theologian, involves solitude, commitment to another, and generativity. This surely applies to the monk in his union with Christ and the Church through
vows.

The elemental solitude of the person is forever. We are, as
God is. We are immortal, as God is. We are unique, as God is.
Granted our being, our immortality, our uniqueness are limited,
they are genuine dimensions of the human. In our life together
with Christ and one another in church and community, we remain unique. This is a truth and not merely accepted, but to be
realistically dealt with. It is an operating function of our being.
We come alone, we depart alone. We live alone, even if in the
bonds of a commitment.

The element of permanent commitment is basic to marriage,
and so too to our love for Christ, his Church, and our community.
Christ loves his spouse and does so forever. Nothing will change
that, even if at times some members be unworthy. So too our love
for him, for his Church, for our community is a binding, a bonding that is beauteous because it is abiding. Divorce and separation
and dispensation notwithstanding, it is the dimension of perma-
nence that is the essential beauty—the fidelity of the individual
to the loving God, spouse of his soul, lover of his heart. We remain forever who we are, engaged in a commitment that is deep
and everlasting, and the union is fruitful for our good and the
good of all.

At Cana Christ gave expression to this. The second sacrament: Baptism, and then human and divine union.

We are not like little old ladies, but, notwithstanding, old
monks enjoy the entrance, the clothing, the vows of the new-

comer. Life goes on. The birth of grandchildren is perhaps a deeper experience for the old couple than it is for the actual parents by reason of years of committed love that was at once solitary, communal, and creative.

Well, no doubt the wine will one day be blood, but we can meanwhile nonetheless rejoice in the Bridegroom who is the source of eternal joy. Amen.

HOLY RECREATION

I came across a text by a sociologist, a study of our monastery in Iowa, an in-depth study that took several years. He devoted his career to an investigation of communities of all kinds, the monastic life one of them.[1]

Describing community life, he came at one point to the matter of recreation. Recreation in common is found in any social group. His first monastic example of that: the monks drop what they are doing and go to choir seven times a day.

I have heard choir spoken of as song and dance, but I don't think I have ever heard it considered recreation. Singing in groups, he wrote, is found everywhere as recreation. With monks it has an added dimension of great meaning, what he calls the asceticism of it. By that he means the spiritual emphasis. The monk not only sings as an enjoyable enterprise but does so as love, as prayer, as worship, as religion.

This is an interesting observation. The author goes on to note the numerous feasts and celebrations of the Church year: Easter, Christmas, and all the rest. The mysteries of Jesus, his Mother, the saints are all considered as recreation.

Perhaps it is because recreation in our culture is so far removed from religious celebration that we find it odd to conceive it otherwise. However, early European drama was the mystery play in the cathedral. The feasts were celebrated not only with Mass and ritual but also with food and drink, dance, market, commerce, procession. The link of religion and celebration was close. People traveled, but often enough on pilgrimage, not mere

---

[1] George Hillery, Jr., *The Monastery: A Study in Freedom, Love, and Community.* Westport, CT: Praeger, 1992.

tourists. The spiritual overtone was significant. The pleasure was also pleasing to God.

Most of our culture's celebrations, our recreation, are far removed from faith and the expression of faith. There is a certain pathos in Louisville resorting to Pegasus as some sort of symbol of the city and the city's cult of the horse. As a pagan mythical figure, Pegasus is at best rather weak. There is no aspect of prayer or worship involved with the Kentucky Derby. It is recreation, indeed, but recreation earthbound and shallow.

There is more sadness in this than mere negative comment. It reveals an attitude, a frame of mind, that so flattens life, robs it of significance in the widest sense, barren of spirit and the transcendent quality that can so lift and inspire the human heart.

Anyone who has known ethnic neighborhoods knows how fiestas of all sorts are part of the people's culture, feasts rooted in faith, but celebrated on earth in song and dance, food and drink, lights and banners.

How odd that a monastery should end up the healthiest enterprise around by way of its integral living: one foot in Heaven and another on earth. We refuse to be silly and superficial. If Heaven is not an aspect of earth there is no truth in it. Then a barren culture turns to the moment of silence as the best it can come up with in terms of celebration, akin to a mute viewing at a wake. How sad.

It is, after all, recreation that we deal with, to renew the earth, to re-create it with God by returning it to its original purpose, the honor and glory of God.

We celebrate the earth in terms of Christ's return to save it, redeem it, glorify it. In prayer and rite, in feast and fast, in procession and in silence, in cowl and cloak, in choir and before the altar, we have the joy of celebrating the point of life. We return to creation and its original point and re-create.

Can there be a greater contribution to a world so impoverished, so blind? Can there be a greater sorrow than being condemned to find the full meaning of life here and here alone? Can we do the world a greater good than opening it up to the transcendent, the immortal, and that by way of song and dance, rite and ritual, ceremony and act?

There goes on all around us, in the military, in community festivals, in sports, what is called "recreation." Into that we plant the eternal note, the relation to God, to eternal life, immortal union with God in our destiny, all of us. Truly a great call, a great call indeed. Amen.

TRUE HEARING AND TRUE SPEECH

Mark 7:31-37

I am sitting in a rocker in the west lounge of the infirmary. The sunset room looks out on the shale country as the sunrise room on the east looks out on the limestone country. I am quietly rocking and reading. Quietly. The phone rings once, twice. Out of his room back of me bounces Brother John, wakened from his nap. He answers, "No. He's not here." And goes back to continue his nap.

I think, how remarkable the human ear. Among other sounds it sorts out only the phone and passes it on to the sleeping brother. So I continue my rocking and reading.

I understand why Jesus would be interested in restoring a man's hearing and, in consequence, his speech. Rather than saying he restored them, may we say, rather, he gave him what he never had. The man had never heard and consequently never spoke. Noises are not speech.

We understand why Jesus took him aside and away from the crowd. The onslaught of sound would no doubt overwhelm him, bewilder the man, maybe frighten him. He would hear the human voice for the first time and, of course, not understand a word. How could he? He would be quite overwhelmed.

So there is more than one miracle here. There are several. Jesus taught him in a moment the mystery of speech. The man not only heard the human voice but understood it. The first voice he heard was that of Jesus.

Nor was that all. His tongue was loosed. He not only understood human speech when he heard it, but he was able to respond. He who never spoke before, who never heard before. A whole series of miracles.

Perhaps you have read, as I did, of the man who lost his sight as a child of three when playing with some chemicals that exploded? Now, nearly 40, he recovers his sight. Sight he has, but he cannot see. He has to learn how to interpret the images his eyes fashion. We learn to see with the gift of sight, a long, slow process. It takes him a while to recognize his wife. He is not sure that trees are but shadows. He is more comfortable skiing with eyes closed than with them open. We must learn to see.

How wonderful the work of Jesus in restoring the man's ability to hear and to speak, then giving the man the ability to use them.

The analogy is not too hidden, the lesson in all this. We have hearing and we have speech. But we may not have the art of hearing, nor the gift of speech, not only with one another but also with God. We need to move on to another kind of hearing and another kind of speech, the inner kind, the spiritual communication.

These are dying arts in our day. The world is overwhelmed with seeing and hearing and becomes unable to see and hear on the deeper level. The inner communication is gone, the line is dead, the inner life is dormant. The world is satisfied with mere seeing and mere hearing. All becomes shallow and superficial, without depth. When people deep by nature become shallow by nurture, we are cultivating the frustrated life in which even a surfeit comes nowhere near satiety.

In which case a monastery that cultivates listening and fosters inner dialogue is about the most significant thing around. It does a finer service to the human scene than is done anywhere by anyone.

It is a work of God, of course. He takes us aside to do it, away from the crowd. Apart. Amen.

OUR IMPRACTICAL LIFE

The Holy Roman Empire originally included what is now Germany, Austria, western Czechoslovakia, Switzerland, eastern France, the Low Countries, and part of Italy. By the time Joseph II, son of Maria Theresa, became Emperor, it was considerably less. He died in 1790 and the Empire not long after. He left his name in history in Josephinism. He tried to make the Church a department of his kingdom, by royal right. He interfered in every area in a gross way.

Cistercians remember him, for he considered monasteries of our sort of no practical value. He got rid of them, 867 in all. They could survive only by doing something Joseph thought practical, so many of them began boarding schools of quality. They still have them. They make up one branch of our Order. We are in the other, having no ministries, no schools, no parishes. We are not practical. Joseph was quite right.

In a word, who needs fruitcake or cheese or fudge for that matter—even with the bourbon? We have no practical value. We are in the category of the arts: opera, ballet, sculpture, painting, song and dance, poetry, daffodils, and hyacinths. What practical value have they?

None. They are of another order than practicality. They pertain to the human spirit, to the transcendent dimension. We are immortal, all. We are destined for an eternal union with God. All of us, not just monks. Not just Catholics. Christians. All. And "God enlightens everyone who comes into this world." All suspect with varying intensity that there is more than this. There is more to follow. This is not the whole story.

And that's what a place like this monastery says. There is indeed more, and we are witnesses to that as a sort of art form. But we are not a dead one. We are no Deerfield Village or Plymouth

Plantation or Shakertown, a reconstructed past on display. We are a living entity, and as Cistercians, over a thousand years old.

We are the whole package of a community of men, committed to love and peace, to work and prayer, to hospitality for the sojourner, under an abbot and a rule. It is all for God. God alone gives the place a meaning. It teaches the heart the way art does on the deep, psychic, spiritual level. Powerfully. Not just the Catholic heart, but the human heart.

For all are immortal and they all know it. When that inner light grows weak and wavering, a place like this gives it new confidence, enhances, increases it. To be sure, any church spire says as much. What meaning has a church except spiritually? That's what it is and what it's for.

But this house does it in a more dramatic way, as all art does. It makes an explicit statement, an exaggerated one, the sort of statement Jesus often made. "If your eye offend you, pluck it out. Better in Heaven with one eye than Hell with two."

Keep the transcendent dimension of your own life burning bright through prayer and sacrament, through love and peace, mercy and justice. It changes every fiber of your being when the transcendent is your priority. Live for God. Nothing else is worth it.

We do worse than make fruitcake. We get up in the night to sing psalms. Indeed, we do it seven times a day. For God. For you. For all. Joseph II was quite right. We have no practical value.

God bless us all. Amen.

FAITHFUL TO THE CORE

John 2:13-22

In 1926, when I was in the fourth grade, the children of the Belcher School in East Milton walked to the square to attend the dedication of a monument to commemorate the first railroad in America. Strictly speaking, it was not the first, but among the first and the best known. It carried thirty-ton granite blocks from the quarry in Quincy three miles to the Neponset River, where barges carried the blocks to Charlestown for the Bunker Hill monument. This, to note the Battle of Bunker Hill 150 years before. The battle was lost to the British, but British losses were so great that they later abandoned Boston.

Down in Baltimore in the later era of canals, the businessmen were concerned that much former produce that once came over the mountains to the coast and cities like Baltimore was lost to the Erie Canal and the Hudson River and the port of New York. They proposed to do something about it and set out to build a railroad like the one they visited in Milton, this one across the mountains to the Ohio River and the nearest city, Wheeling, West Virginia. It took years to set this venture up, but by 1852 the Irish workers had reached Wheeling for the Baltimore and Ohio Railroad.

Then, a few years later, when Archbishop Spalding, a local son and head of the Diocese of Baltimore, came for the 1866 dedication of Gethsemani's church, he came by train from Wheeling to Cincinnati, where he no doubt paused in the rigors of travel with his brother, Archbishop Purcell of Cincinnati, and then went on to Louisville. There he met Bishop Lavalle and came on the Nashville line to Gethsemani station.

Surely local leaders took their best carriages to meet the prelates and the many guests that came with them. It was a great day. Not only was the wilderness graced by a sizeable Catholic population, with a former cathedral of splendid beauty in Bardstown, though the bishop was now located in Louisville, but the Abbey of Gethsemani was dedicating a most handsome abbey church. This was worth noting.

If talk among the guests would have centered on the new abbey church, it would also have dealt with the wonder of modern travel. No doubt many details would have been shared of the journey through the mountains, the long trip along the Ohio, the stops made. And above all, the speed. We today might forget that the step was from horse, to horse and buggy, to train. Going from a few miles an hour to forty or fifty miles an hour was amazing. The train was the fastest thing in the universe, an achievement also worth noting. In fact, the Civil War was the first war in which the railroad played a significant role.

The prelates and the priests and the monks and the people must have felt very much alive, indeed rather excited about the achievements of the country. The war, thank God, was over and the rebuilding of America was underway. This church in the wilderness was a blessed sign that God was with us.

The monks followed tradition and built in the usual pattern of the basilica: the long nave, the apse. This takes us back to the early church in Rome. The fact that we are a minor basilica is true. It is a basilica and we do have ties with the earliest Roman church. But it is also American.

The design was very American and followed the popular pattern of having a roof lined with lath and plaster and creating arches and bays later painted to make the whole something of a Gothic church. This was done everywhere. It could be called "poor man's Gothic" since few could afford stone churches, let alone arches and bays. Like the statues made of plaster, one did what one could with what one had. The general effect was pleasing, and the manner is still popular.

There is inherent in the Cistercian inheritance a trend toward the authentic. This goes back to our first monastery at Citeaux where the young monks were captivated by the possibility of being monks in as authentic a way as possible. It involved shedding accretions and reaching the original that became characteristic of the Cistercian.

Thus, it was to be taken for granted that sooner or later the lath and the plaster would come down, and we would give up trying to look like something we were not, and become what we really are. So, in time the original church emerged, and we are so taken by those who erected so superb a structure. We pardon that early generation for trying to be more American than there was need to be. We can understand that. Every people coming here—and we have all come from somewhere else—has tried to adapt and fit and be localized, even if much of that was not necessary. In the end we become Americans by loyalty to our best traditions.

So today we rejoice in a handsome church our forefathers created in far-off Kentucky. Nor is the lesson lost on us. Our efforts to adjust, to adapt, to be part of our time and an aspect of our culture, must nonetheless remain authentic to what we are and profess to be. This is a never-done project; it is a continuing project.

Yes, we have cars and trucks and all-terrain vehicles. We have coolers and air conditioning. We have heat and computers and web pages. We ship UPS and Parcel Post. We fly to Rome and anywhere else. We have top medical care. But the core, the heart, the point is still there, and we mean to keep it there. We still get up in the night to chant and do so seven times a day. We still have an abbot and a Rule and obey both. We wear the same habit our fathers wore and make the same vows and try to keep them. Anyone from the past could join us and with a bit of adjustment feel at home. Those archbishops coming by train surely made the papers. They themselves were quite excited by it. For all that, we too are quite excited to be alive, to be here, to be monks, in this church, this year.

Amen.

A GREAT MAN OF GOD

Matthew 5:13-16

Michael Casey, a monk of Tarrawarra Abbey in Yarra Glen, Victoria, Australia, had a fine article on Saint Bernard in the two-volume *Encyclopedia of Monasticism*. In it he notes that for some time Bernard was dismissed as a lightweight theologically, given to gushy spiritual writing, something of a gadabout for a monk, into everything, knew everyone, not to forget preaching a Crusade against the Turks that was a fiasco. I grew up in that period of Bernard's assessment.

Then Étienne Gilson, in 1934, wrote *The Mystical Theology of Saint Bernard*. It was the beginning of a new look at Saint Bernard. Indeed, the beginning of a complete reversal. Gilson, you recall, was mentor to Dan Walsh, and Dan Walsh was mentor to Father Louis (Thomas Merton) and was the providential inspiration for the man's coming to Gethsemani.

As Merton was a Bernard on a small scale, we can pass through him to some grasp of the medieval saint's impact on history. It is simplest to see him as a man of God, an obvious working of a very special Providence.

The facts and figures are staggering and well known. The Order had only ten monasteries when the *Carta Caritatis* was approved in 1119. By the time Bernard died this day in 1153, it had 351 abbeys, half of them in France, 169 of them attached to Clairvaux.

That, of course, is only to touch on the total impact of the man on his time. He went everywhere and was into everything of significance. Remember, travel was by walking or by horse, one not much faster than the other. If there were roads, they were not always apt for any sort of carriage or wagon. Communication was by letter, carried by whatever method possible. There were not even clocks to tell the time, save water clocks of cavalier accuracy.

In other words, he was a phenomenon. So, we reach the inevitable conclusion. This is more than human design. The hand of God is here. Loud and clear. With emphasis.

The Cistercian explosion that followed, sprinkling Europe with hundreds of abbeys, of monks and nuns, is really unbelievable. The abbeys were not shacks or shanties or trailer parks, but beautiful structures following Bernard's pattern. Many of them are still extant. They were not thrown up, somehow, but the fruit of a decade or two of skilled labor, monastic and lay.

Which brings us to today and our own time. Have we ever had a pope like John Paul II? Even as a man of his own time and therefore familiar with every technique of communication, he is none the less extraordinary. By whatever standard, has he an equal?

If Roosevelt, Churchill, Gandhi, Teresa are great in some sense, this man's greatness equals, even outdistances them.

God has visited us in our time in a most dramatic way, and we have been witnesses to it. It has happened in our day and we are part of it.

If we celebrate Bernard, and we do, it is because he represented God acting in history, in the human scene, making an impact that is still with us.

Don't be so blind, then, as not to see that same God in our own day, in our own circumstances, promoting the cause of God and humankind. Let your joy over Bernard be reflected in your joy over John Paul, for God is with us.

As small minds nibbled on Bernard to demean him, so today some are so small as to mislabel John Paul. It figures.

The world is much a mess, and who would deny it? Rather, see the working of God in our time, our scene, and take heart. The Cistercian heart takes joy in Bernard the Magnificent. The Catholic heart sees the same God raising up in our midst a great man of God as He did for us in Bernard. The one helps us see the other for what he is.

Amen.

I AM A KING

Luke 23:35-43

I am standing at the entrance of the piazza of St. Peter's in Rome, and someone next to me, pointing to the basilica, says, "What's all this got to do with the humble Jesus of Nazareth?"

And I say to him in reply, "Everything. It has everything to do with the humble Jesus of Nazareth!"

All you need do, of course, is to recall Jesus before Pilate, Jesus in the most desperate situation of his life, at best a pathetic figure. He is asked by the Roman authority if he is a king. "I am a king," he answered, a statement one would think bordering on madness, or at least severe delusion.

And yet . . . and yet, he is a king because he said so. He is the Son of God, for he said so. He is God Almighty, Lord of Heaven and Earth.

So I said to my neighbor in front of St. Peter's, "That magnificent mass is a pathetic endeavor to say of Jesus that he is the Son of God." True enough. How do you express a belief in the divinity of Christ?

You do it any way you can: in word, in song, in rite, in performance, in art of whatever kind. Look around you. How do people want to be reckoned significant? They build big houses, mansions, palaces, estates. These say something. Egyptian Pharaohs built pyramids lest they be forgotten. Former Presidents build libraries and museums and centers commemorating their deeds in a handful of years in the White House. People write books and climb mountains so they will be remembered.

Every diocese has at least one splendid church, and that is the cathedral. The diocese may have many parish churches, perhaps most of them of no great account. But, there is always the cathedral.

The President lives in a splendid house, has a private jet, is treated the rest of his life with honors quite special. What else can you do?

If the Church is everywhere in the world, and it is, it is also among the poor. Go anywhere and find works of mercy. We need explicit expressions of love for Christ as God, so that we can keep alive the faith that sees Christ and God in everyone. Sometimes a church is the only beautiful thing the poor have, and the love of the poor for the Lord is surely some of the most beautiful worship he receives.

A symphony, opera, ballet, museums, and art forms of every sort are essential to us because we are spiritual beings, so the beauty of worship in a beautiful structure is basic, worldwide, all through time.

We did not give Christ the title of king. He did. He is a king. He does reign. He has a Kingdom. To give expression to that is difficult. We are a poor people, helpless in trying to say something that cannot be said.

What can you as a monk do for a king? You can honor him. You can serve him. You can love him. And you do. Yet, we are so limited in all that.

Hence, we build churches and monasteries. We create a form of life. It involves how we live, where we live, what we eat, what we wear, what we do. The whole is a way of making love. What does it have to do with Jesus of Nazareth? It has everything to do with him. We take what we are, what we have, what we can do, and we make love with it. It is all we can do.

Ask anyone, "How do you make love?" It is as good an answer as any to say, "We build St. Peter's, or a monastery, or a gatehouse."

That Jesus of Nazareth is a king we know and believe. You are pledged to serve him in his Kingdom, in your own heart, in your brother, in this house, the place, the time that is ours. All of it has everything to do with Jesus of Nazareth.

Amen.

FANTASY VERSUS REALITY

Matthew 14:22-33

Buddy Ballard used to work at the alfalfa complex on the hill. We called it the de-hy for the dehydrating process in making pellets from alfalfa. Buddy had a red convertible, a Ford, I think, with top down all summer—very smart, very sporty for the mid-'60s. I used to work up there with Brother Gerlac.

One day things were in a mess and, in the midst of it, Brother asked me if I would run down to the Post Office and see if the spare part had come. "Sure. Buddy, why don't I use your convertible?" "OK, go ahead."

So I zoomed down the hill and up the front avenue with work scapular blowing in the wind, like Isadora Duncan. I came to a dramatic stop at the gatehouse and, standing there, just having come, were three impressive ladies, looking like queen mothers, big-bosomed dowagers. They gave me a haughty going over, obviously distressed at this display. I ran into the Post Office, got the package, and ran out. They were still standing there with long faces like El Greco. I waved at them, pointed to the red convertible, and said, "Pretty nice, huh?"

They were not amused. "We thought you'd be in your cloister." I had no time and scooted off, leaving total disillusionment behind me. I had not measured up to their notions of a monk of Gethsemani, 1965. They were very vexed.

I frequently had occasion years ago to be in on it when Father Louis would meet someone or other, usually in connection with vocation work. It was interesting to note how many were frankly disappointed with the real Thomas Merton. Not all, but many. They had their own idea of what he must be like but, when confronted with his person, were at a loss to adjust to the reality. He was so bland.

Indeed, at his very last appearance, as it were, when he gave that last conference in Bangkok, two monks who heard him to the end were not impressed. In the blunt way of scholars, one said to the other, "Well, that wasn't much." Maybe it wasn't in terms of what the monks expected, no doubt some dazzling performance that would leave all breathless and on their feet with applause. He had not measured up to expectations. It happens all the time. To me. To you.

John the Baptist sent a delegation, asking, "Are you he who is to come or do we look for another?" Possibly John had his doubts. Far more likely is it that the questions were put for the benefit of the hesitant, the perplexed. Jesus answered them by showing how the Scriptures described the man of God who was to come, "The blind see, the deaf hear, the lame walk, the dead are raised to life, and the poor have good news preached to them." They could draw their own conclusions.

Presumably they did. We know from history that the majority concluded that he did not measure up to expectations. They rejected him. They had their own ideas of what made a Messiah and it was up to any Messiah to conform. His problem. Not theirs.

Strong stands like that are dangerous. They have great power. They are so likely to lead to action. They led to the death of Jesus.

A sure sign that you or I are engaging in the same dynamics of trying to adjust reality to fantasy is anger. Anger is the giveaway, the tell-tale. Especially hidden anger. Resentment.

I think it is something we all know in the course of a life. We have all been disappointed. Men often marry an illusion. Only later do they meet their wife, hopefully come to know her and love her. The man she marries may not exist save in her dreams. It can be difficult learning to love reality.

How many of you found here what you expected? The older you are and the longer here, the more easy it is to say with certainty, not one of you knew what you were getting into. How could you have? No one could have guessed ahead of time what happened here the last twenty years, or any twenty years, or in any life. Ask one of the neighbors, has life been as you expected?

So, of necessity, somewhere along the line, you dropped fantasy and began to love reality. Your notions of the monastic life were all in your head, written in a book you read. They had no contact with the real. If you did not abandon your fantasies and enter into loving union with reality, well, it is no great insight to say you are an unhappy man and a man of anger.

You have been disappointed. The reality did not measure up to your expectations. You are like the dowagers in the avenue who were indignant at a monk who did not behave as they thought he ought. In a way, they did not deserve an explanation or get one. I did not tell them that it was not my convertible, or even the monastery's, or that we worked outside the cloister as well as in.

Thomas Merton was a constant annoyance to many in and out of the monastery because he catered to no one's pious delusions. Even now it is amusing to ask someone how soon they think Merton will be canonized and the 10th of December become his feast day? It is not the merit of the case which is the issue. The very idea strikes those who knew him as ridiculous. Their faces cloud in distress at the very idea. Their notion of sanctity and Merton have nothing in common.

I take the matter seriously. Not Merton and the Bangkok conference, nor me and the visiting ladies, but you and me and Jesus. If we are not willing and able to give all away in our relationship to God, to God's service, to the Kingdom of Heaven, we are in very dangerous waters. We shall never know freedom nor the joy this Sunday celebrates. We may program our Jesus and expect Him to conform to our program, but he will honor it only by ignoring it.

The dearest thing to me in the monastic life I came to was the Latin office. I make no bones about it. It had everything. One morning I woke to find that it was gone. They did not even bother to ask me first! What we have in its place is something else, but for all its beauty, a poor thing to what it replaced. The lesson is a good one for me. The love of God and his service is beyond anything you can lay claim to. You meet God as he comes, and he comes as he pleases, when he pleases. If you are not willing to meet him on those terms, you will never meet him. Then you will have to be content with the fantasy Jesus you have made for yourself, who is not real, in whom there is no salvation.

"Art thou he who is to come, or shall we look for another?"

Amen.

IS GOD LESS CREATIVE THAN MAN?

Matthew 2:1-12

In the summer of 1939, at the end of college and on my way home before entering the Divine Word Society novitiate, I made a brief visit to the World's Fair in New York City. World War II had already begun, but the affair was well attended and very impressive. Russia had a huge display, so did Italy. One of the most popular was Bell Telephone.

On the front wall of a great hall was a huge map of the United States, major cities noted with light. Across the front of the bare room was a counter with several hundred phones. On the stage above were two phones, used in turn. The idea was that you could call anywhere in the country free. Just line up and take your turn. On the many phones up front, others could listen. It was a take-off on the old custom of listening in on a party line.

So, the volunteer would give a number—say, in Seattle. A light would go on in New York City, and soon after a line of light would extend to Buffalo, after a few moments to Toledo. Then the line of light would move on to Chicago, then Des Moines, and so on across the country, until the line reached Seattle where the phone would ring and a dialogue would begin. "Aunt Minnie, this is Brendan." And so on. "Minnie, take care. I'm in New York City at the World's Fair and there are about 200 people listening."

It was a clever bit, a marvel. Fancy! A line of wire across the country—hundreds of wires really—and you can get on one and reach anywhere. It was thought a remarkable achievement. And it was, 67 years ago. We have moved along some since.

It is no great feat to accept the Gospel story of the incarnation. If humans can do what they do, it is possible that God could make angels, shepherds, Bethlehem, a star and wise men from the East. If people can do marvels, and they can, so can God, one assumes.

One of our neighbors was at Mass on Epiphany years ago, in the chapel at 6:00 A.M. with his children. The priest was sympathetic with his worshippers and said, in effect, "You know, it is good to be clear. The point of this holy season is that God became man and came to live with us. This is the issue. The details we may not be sure of, save the Virgin birth. But choirs of angels, the shepherds, the star in the night, and even the visit of the kings is something else again. It is good to keep a sense of balance."

Well, as could be expected, our neighbor was not buying it. He was upset. "Why do priests have to spoil Christmas for children by spouting those theories?" So he came to me, later.

My answer was—in terms of what men and women have achieved even in my lifetime—I find it no problem at all that God is quite capable of something as beautiful as the song of angels, wise men from the East, guided by a star, coming to worship the Son of God.

I'm a monk, you know. I'm involved in things like cloister and abbot and a rule of life, celibacy and obedience, cowls and candles, refectory and chapter room, bells and incense, most of which mean little to many people.

To me it is all beautiful and to be involved is pure gift. It is a witness to the beauty of God and so is a boon to our neighbors and our world. All of it speaks of God as much or more than stars do, or the songs of birds, the laughter of a child, the love of a man or woman. It is all a witness to beauty and a solace to all whom it touches, a sharing of the incarnation, a journey with the Magi.

Amen.

MYSTERIES OF FAITH AND LIFE

Hp/21

46 98 18

OUR JUST DESSERTS?

Matthew 9:9-13

What is considered Abraham Lincoln's finest piece of oratory is inscribed on the south wall of the interior of the Lincoln Memorial in Washington, the Second Inaugural Address. On the opposite wall is the Gettysburg Address.

In the Second Inaugural Lincoln made some amazing statements about the Civil War, then coming to an end.

> The Almighty has his own purposes. "Woe unto the world because of offenses! For it must needs be that offenses come. But woe to that man by whom the offense cometh!" If we shall suppose that American slavery is one of those offenses which, in the Providence of God, must needs come, but which, having continued through his appointed time, He now wills to remove, and that He gives to both North and South, this terrible war, as the woe due to those by whom the offense came, shall we discern therein any departure from those divine attributes which the believers in a Living God always ascribe to Him?

In an address to an Indian regiment several days later he said,

> Fondly do we hope—fervently we pray—that this mighty scourge of war may speedily pass away. Yet, if God wills that it continue, until all the wealth piled by the bondman's two hundred and fifty years of unrequited toil shall be sunk, and until every drop of blood drawn with the lash, shall be paid by another drawn with the sword, as was said three thousand years ago, so still it must be said, "the judgments of the Lord are true and righteous altogether."

Is war, then, a scourge for our sins? Was Hitler a punishment for the Germans, Stalin for the Russians, Mussolini for the Italians?

Roosevelt and Hitler were contemporaries, both elected by their people. Did each people get what they deserved?

The Irish and the Polish are not the only people with a wretched history. Did they merit it? Were the people of Tibet deserving of their country being destroyed by the Chinese?

It would seem complex questions are not satisfied with simplistic answers. We believe in a God of history, the Lord of time, Divine Providence. But when it comes to specifics we do not have enough data to formulate an answer.

Perhaps Lincoln could not say what he said today, any more than evangelists were able to say that September 11 and the fall of the World Trade Center was the result of our sins. The most we can say is that sin has its own sequel, and all the evil we know stems from sin. However, we cannot apply the rule to specifics. The rain falls on good and evil alike. So does the hail. So do bombs. A good life does not necessarily follow a moral one, nor a bad life an immoral one. The matter is a mystery, deep and complex.

One could say that Catholics deserve what they get in their priests, but the statement is gratuitous. The first twelve picked by Jesus give a good lesson. They were chosen by the Son of God. One of them was a disreputable man named Matthew. It would seem that more than appearances are involved. We really do not know much about the deeps of life. That you and I are here, were called here, asks more questions than it answers.

But this response is clear enough, and Lincoln gave it.

> With malice toward none, with charity for all, with firmness in the right as God gives us to see the right, let us strive to finish the work we are in, to bind up the nation's wounds, to care for him who shall have borne the battle, and for his widow and his orphan, to do all which may achieve and cherish a just and lasting peace among ourselves and with all nations.

Words that could be written in gold. Fitting when said. Fitting today. This we can fully understand and respond to. Here all is clarity. There is no point in a question with no answer. Clear answers call for a response that rises from clear conviction.

TRUST IN GOD'S MERCY

Matthew 11:25-30

Once, in an off-hand remark, Father Louis (Thomas Merton) said to me, a novice under his direction, "You're superstitious." This was in response to some comment I had made. There's some truth in it. Sometimes I interpret things in what I see as an attitude of faith, but which in reality is perhaps not faith at all. Perhaps this is a Celtic tendency.

Take those troubled priests, most of them adult victims themselves of some early abuse. Now men of God, daily at the altar, hearing confessions, doing the Gospel, tripped up, caught by their own flawed story.

I do not imply innocence, or see failure in responsibility not a fault, or ignore the evil involved, the harm done. I just find it mysterious.

There are 50,000 victims of sexual abuse in Kentucky, according to a University of Kentucky poll a few years ago. Some of them became priests. Probably the past was never mentioned or noted, just a past hidden or denied, as is, or was, the usual approach. The great denial shared by our society.

Then it caught up with them, betrayed them, and by an amalgam of events all was revealed. The revelation became a wildfire that spread among an amazed people. Unthinkable. Unheard of. Never dreamed.

Abraham Lincoln in his Second Inaugural Address attributed the Civil War to God's response to the evil of slavery. It would seem that his view was acceptable. But, when some evangelists attributed the New York tragedy of September 11 to an act of God in reprisal for our sins, there was an outbreak of outrage that men of God would say such a thing. So, they withdrew their statements with apology in a few days.

Here comes my Irish superstition again. Are these guilty priests victims for the rest of us, expressions of God's displeasure at American morals or, if you will, American Catholic morals? Is the shortage of priests something we had coming, that we don't deserve them if we pay small heed to them?

Since I am troubled by these thoughts, I have to deal with them. I do not assume you have similar thoughts, but such a thought might have flashed through your mind for a moment or two.

Can we read God into such tragic events as these? I don't think so. It is not that simple. Reading the mind of God is not that easy.

So, instead of looking out, I look in. Rather than look at the sad failure in others, I look at sad failure within me and see in sorrow and suffering some result I helped bring about by my own sin. Who of us is without sin?

Then I take the next step and ask for God's mercy, on me and on everyone else. I pray to God to accept all suffering in this world and my own modest share in it as a sorrow for sin. We are united to the merciless death we inflicted on a merciful Lord.

I do not see such prayers as idle or a mere gesture. They are an expression, not of guilt, for I trust my sins are forgiven, but of repentance, an act of compunction. We all so need the mercy of God, and we do so need to trust in it for us and for all.

This cannot be assumed as already in action. Otherwise God would not raise a saint in our day and officially canonize her, whose entrance in prayer into the psyche of our time led her to espouse the mercy of God in a dynamic way and encouraged others to do the same. Her efforts were blessed by the Church. She saw a great need of trust in God's mercy. If Faustina were not enough, we have Padre Pio and his bearing the very wounds of Christ in a union of love.

So the suffering of these priests does not so much make them victim souls immolated for themselves and all of us. Rather, they give us one more taste of the human scene. Our beautiful world and our beautiful people, not to say our beautiful children, are all touched by the darkness of evil. Against that there is no hope save in the grace of God and the mercy of God.

That is my response when I fear the hand of God has touched us: God have mercy on us. Amen.

TRACES OF THE TRINITY

John 16:12-15

In the religious myths of people in all parts of the world, God becoming human is common enough. Even if the fulfillment of these aspirations was something wholly beyond imagination, the very thrust of them says much about human nature and the quest for some participation in God. The first reaction to the discovery that many of our fundamental religious truths have been not merely echoes but even close counterparts in other religions, even in what we call false religions, was a kind of disillusionment. Is our faith, too, just another dream? Is Christmas just an updated primitive celebration of the winter solstice?

Later it came home to us that our faith is strongly affirmed by these spiritual insights, many of them profound. Far from being alien to human nature, our faith is rather wholly consistent, consonant with it. It is so much so that one can say that if the impossible were possible, we would have invented the faith had it not been revealed, so proper to us is it.

The virgin birth, Jesus as God and human, his death at our hands, his resurrection from the dead, his ascension into Heaven, his calling us after him—these realities are not diminished because they were the mystical yearnings of so much of mankind, the dreams and desires of the human soul. Rather, they are all the more emphasized. That these divine mysteries are rooted in history, are not poetic figments, becomes their ultimate distinction and greatest power. They happened. It is all true.

If then the dualities so common in our thinking, God and humanity, heaven and hell, time and eternity, body and soul, male and female, interior and exterior are accepted without

difficulty as terms for revelation too, how much more amazing
is it that the most sublime of religious truths, that of the Holy
Trinity, should also have been stumbled on in some way long
before the truth was fully known. The idea of a triune God is not
unknown in other religious cultures. This truth satisfies something in us, has an appeal touching something deep down.

It is possible to consider how people might have wondered
whether trinity was not found in God. That duality leads to union
we know well enough, and then this union to something new, a
third. Body and soul form the human. You are not body, you are
not soul, nor are you body and soul together, but a new third,
the human.

Vision is not possible without duality. Having two eyes is
essential if one is to know more than the flat world of the new-
born, to know distance, perspective. Only two ears make possible
a hearing that is complete, taking in the whole aspect of sound.
You cannot by sound locate an airplane flying overhead if you
have but one ear, for you lack the coordinates. Thus, even our
hearing and our vision, though dual, bring a third into being
because the fruit of sight is the exact point to which they lead.
Sound is stereophonic, that is, three-dimensional, embodied.
Sight is stereoscopic, three-dimensional, two plus one.

Fullness and the whole take two hands. We sense this when
we grasp something with both hands. We then feel we have a
hold on our subject, in many senses. One hand extended to another is a commercial deal, a military pact, something civil. But
a handshake is not an act of love. If we love someone we use two
hands, two arms. Pope Paul VI embraced Athenagoras. He did
not merely shake hands with him like at the Rotary or Kiwanis.
So two leads to three, two hands make real a relationship, something new, a third.

The fruit of human love is a child, a new third born of love.
Indeed, within the person, celibate or espoused, the union of
opposites within brings about the development and full flower
of the mature person, neither male nor female, but Christ-like,
androgynous, the full person, the new third.

Pondering these notions, as humans have done since time
began, could well enough lead to a consideration of a God—sole,
singular, who generated another and in union with him knew a

third who was one of them, as in sight, in sound, in touch, in love, in maturity.

We sometimes think that the whole mystery of the Trinity is so profound a truth—it is the most profound in Christianity—that considering it is best left to professional theologians. Yet it was monks who first celebrated it liturgically. Even people who did not know revelation have seen in threeness something fascinating and divine. Frank Sheed, who for years preached to all comers in the open air in parks and squares and street corners, said that more questions were asked about the Holy Trinity than any other subject.

This feast of the Holy Trinity, then, made a matter of observance for the whole Church by Pope John XXII in 1334, is a call to us to probe this holy mystery. The singular is so often dual, and duality so often leads to a new third, which is in turn the fruit of the two found in the one.

O holy and undivided Trinity, one God, the Father, Son, and Holy Spirit, to whom be glory and honor forever and ever.

It is in Christ that we not merely contemplate this sublime mystery but truly enter into it, share it, adopted of the Father in Christ by the Spirit given us. If the Christian experience is what we seek, rather than theological investigation, this is the awareness brought home to us today, why as monks we celebrate it. Through Christ in the Spirit we come before the Father. As sight, sound, a touch, human love, maturity, so we, in Christ, by the Spirit, to the Father. Amen.

COINCIDENCE? OR ANGELS?

This is September. By an old tradition, September is the month of the Holy Angels. The feast of the Archangels, Michael, Gabriel, and Raphael, is on the 29th, though to be sure, that of the Guardian Angels does not appear until early October.

How great the impact of the angels is on contemporary piety, I do not know. The article on "Angels" in Michael Downey's *Dictionary of Christian Spirituality* has a rather diffident approach to the subject, though the book as such seems to be traditional. The *Catechism*, however, is clear enough, even though brief in its coverage. Scripture and tradition have consistently served as adequate support for the angelic world. St. Bernard, among others, is outstanding in his love for the angels. Common piety—even non-Catholic varieties—keeps to the angels, at least to go by published material.

I will tell you a story, a story that is in a way a typical story from the Louisville *Courier-Journal*. It can no doubt be met with a story of your own, an event that has no satisfactory answer save the intercession of angels.

A soldier is going home for Thanksgiving from his base in North Carolina, headed for a town near Fort Knox. He knows he needs gas when he leaves but does nothing about it, thinking he will fill up somewhere along the way. He is deep into night on the Blue Grass Parkway before he begins to worry about his fuel. Of course, he finds no station open at that hour of the night. In a long wooded area, wholly unsettled, so common along thruways, he runs out of gas. He gets out and with his flashlight hopes to signal some car or truck to stop and help him. In a few moments he hears a woman calling for help. His first reaction is that it is a trick of some sort, a ruse. She keeps calling.

He has stopped, he now notes, by the side of a deep gorge or gully, and the woman has somehow driven off the highway and down into this low ground. He can make out the bulk of a car in the dark. Meanwhile, a truck stops and the two go to look. A car is turned over on its side, the woman thrown out, and her legs pinned beneath it. She does not seem seriously hurt, but she cannot move. Eventually, they find help, get the woman off to adequate care, and look to the matter of the soldier having no gasoline.

The driver, as might be expected, is wholly shaken by the experience and concludes with finality that it was the work of angels. It is the only satisfactory answer to how he would happen to run out of gas on a lonely stretch of highway precisely at the spot where this woman had driven off the road into a deep gully, out of sight, and hopelessly pinned there for hours until this driver happened to stop there. The soldier's conclusion, and mine for that matter, is that angels are involved. It is certainly as good an answer as saying that it was a coincidence.

There is a God, and there are angels.

But if one responds, "If that were so, there would be no accidents," the person misses the point. It is the occasional interference that makes the point.

Christ did not heal all lepers, only a few. He did not raise all the dead, only a few. He did not heal all the diseased, only a few. Now and then. Here and there. Yes, but enough to let it be known that something is going on here and you had better take note of it.

There is no point in asking, "Where were angels at the World Trade Center or in New Orleans?" Take care. For all we know, he or they may have been at both. The data are lacking.

It is like the proprietor of Windows on the World at the top of the World Trade Center as he comes to work. Almost there, on impulse, he drops into a jeweler to check his crooked glasses. While he is at it, the building collapses. His restaurant is gone forever, and he alone is left to tell.

I think it is silly to try to come up with conclusive answers to the hand of God or the lack of it in what happens—good or bad—day by day.

I would rather see the world of angels as an aspect of God's beauty and loveliness, not to say his care for the world. The conflict of good and evil—for there are bad angels and good—goes on in every heart at some level or other. The outcome of the struggle is significant. This battle goes on all the time, in everyone, everywhere, and I am sure the angels, good and bad, are involved. Since I love the good and the beautiful, as you love the good and beautiful, I am certain God is on our side.

This is the joy of the angelic world—their magnificence, their number, their power, who dared to show themselves in their love for Jesus at his coming in Mary, in Bethlehem, at the Jordan, in the desert, in Gethsemani, at the Rising, and where else and when.

I am sure they are close to us, to Gethsemani Abbey, to Kentucky and our land, the world, as ever they were. That should be a joy to us.

If God "loves the beautiful warmth of your heart's fire"—and he does—the angels do too. Amen.

PONDER THE GREAT MYSTERIES OF THE FAITH

Matthew 17:1-9

In preparation for the coming disaster of his passion, the Lord took, as it were, his abbot, prior, and subprior—Peter, James, and John—to a high mountain and there to converse with Moses and Elias. He talked of what lay ahead in Jerusalem, meanwhile revealing some of his divine glory to the three. It was an overwhelming scene, and if the text says they fell asleep, it is perhaps not too wide of the mark to say that they were completely overcome.

All of this to encourage them, for not long after he told them what was to happen to him. Then the memorable scene when Peter scolded the Lord and insisted that nothing like that could or should happen. The Lord replied to Peter in strong terms, "Get behind me, Satan. You are wide of the mark." Of the vision on the mount, no word is to be spoken on it until he was raised from the dead.

From our point of view the venture on the mountain was not too successful in achieving its point. Of the three, Peter did not do well. Of James, we know only that he fled, he disappeared. The hero is John, with the Lord to the end.

To display the Transfigured Christ at Easter on a banner in our church is then quite fitting and carries lessons. Granted it came nowhere near the glory and triumph of the Resurrection, it was nonetheless unforgettable.

As good Christians we have no problem with the Lord's rising. We accept it whole and entire and see no need to soften it in any way to make it more palatable.

As John Updike put it,

> Let us not mock God with
> metaphor,
> analogy, sidestepping
> transcendence:
> making the event a parable, a
> sign
> painted in the faded credulity
> of an earlier age:
> Let us walk through the door.

Which leads to the point. It is extremely healthy to enter deeply into the great mysteries of our faith, that is, the outrageous truths we are called upon to accept and embrace. Simple truths, like our immortality—everyone's immortality—that Christ is God and human, present in the Eucharist and offered there till the end of time, the holiness of the priesthood, the life of grace in the sacraments, the beauty of love and life—the whole thing. To ponder these, dwell on these, is superbly healthy for soul and body. To be enchanted with the very extravagance of them all. How healing to live in such deeps, and how much a blessing for the world.

The point is, of course, that we do that now, in this world, this time, this day, with eyes wide open, with total exposure to the slough of misery. We live in a world replete with the ugliness of hate, of violence, and rapine, a world of greed and envy. You need not read the papers, just glance at them. Even blessed as we are with no television, we know all we can handle.

Do you handle all? Wouldn't that be the point? I mean, is your Christianity, your faith, only for good times and good people? Or is your self-knowledge so slight that you do not suspect that you are kin to all these people, blood brothers and sisters?

So your resurrection follows a passion and unhappily the passion is not done yet, nor the rising. We must in some way be disciples of the Passion, Death, and Rising. All or nothing.

We were given Transfiguration to prepare for the Passion, that we might move on into the Rising. There is no harm in recalling that Transfiguration Day is Hiroshima Day. Our day.

Happy Easter, then embrace yourself, your brother, your world, in Christ, and do so with the privilege that is yours for knowing. Amen.

THREE KINDS OF WAITING

Mark 1:1-8

When I was a little boy I would sometimes ride with my father to his shop. To get there we had to cross a large, busy old bridge over the Neponset River on the road from Boston to Qunicy.

Often enough I would see a woman standing at one end of the bridge watching traffic coming out of Boston, looking into each car. I asked my father one day, "What is she waiting for?" He told me, "She is waiting for her son to come back from the war." The war was long over and we were into the 1920s, but she was still waiting. Her mind must have snapped. To a child it seemed a wrenching sadness. That's one kind of waiting.

Along the coast of New England, in fishing towns and villages, sea captains in the days of the clipper ships built big homes. Often enough, on the roof, would be a glassed-in cupola, or a small railed veranda or walk called "the widow's peak" or "the widow's walk." There the wife of the captain would watch her husband sail off to sea, and there she would watch for his return when she received word that he was about due after being so long gone. That is another kind of waiting.

The first kind is futile, done for love, but done in vain. The watched-for son does not exist. There are those who wait and wait in vain for something not real.

The second kind is a waiting that may end happily and may not. The captain and his ship may have gone down off South America months ago. Gone for months, even years, he may yet return and come into view, a passing vessel having brought word of his soon arriving. It is a waiting that may end in heartbreak or may end in rejoicing.

There is a third kind of waiting with which we are concerned. Our waiting involves past and present and what is to come. For Christ has come, he is coming, and he will come again, all mixed together. We wait for one who has already arrived. We exult in his presence. We dream of his return, for he will come again.

This is a relationship to reality that is quite other. This is unique. Here is a mystery and thus a dealing with the mystic sense of reality. Here we can contradict what passes for common sense and yet pass beyond sense to a deeper reality.

How healthy and nurturing such a waiting, such an entry into the wide world of time meeting eternity. It is because we are immortal that such leaps of faith are so sound and so empowering. Through the pondering of such wild ventures we touch the deepest dimensions of our humanity and awaken to the world of time and eternity, earth and Heaven.

While some might dismiss our ventures as a trip into fantasy, we would insist that, on the contrary, we refuse to live in an unreal world that can see and believe only what is in front of it, what makes sense, what adds up.

Besides, we are rooted in history. He fulfilled the promises: born of a woman, in Bethlehem of Judea, in the reign of Herod; suffered, died, and was buried when Pontius Pilate was governor.

We are no distraught woman checking the Boston traffic coming over a bridge for her son returning from war. Nor are we some lonely sea-captain's wife, patiently scanning the horizon for sight of her man's ship coming into view far out to sea.

Rather, we await the promised One whose coming we are witness to: His coming in time, his coming to each of us, his coming at the end in the glory of the new earth, the new Heaven.

Adveniat regnum tuum! Thy Kingdom come!

Come, Lord Jesus. Amen.

A GLORIOUS PRELUDE

Mark 9:2-10

The Transfiguration has never figured mightily in the worship of the Church. For a long time August 6 was just here and there, not always observed. Then at Belgrade a victory in battle with the Turks who were invading Europe occurred. News of it reached Rome on August 6. Pope Calixtus III made the feast of the Transfiguration universal in memory of the event in 1457. We have our own association with the feast, since that was also the day the first atom bomb was released on Hiroshima by American forces. The Gospel reading on the Transfiguration, Mark 9:2-10, has long been read on the second Sunday in Lent.

When I was a child, our family would go to Provincetown on the tip of Cape Cod for a weekend a couple of times each summer. We would stay at a boarding house Friday and Saturday nights and spend all day at the beach. Having a tent was very practical as a place to change for a swim and to get out of the sun and wind once in a while.

So, the idea that Peter suggested three tents or shelters or booths on Mount Tabor makes sense. It would be windy, even on a small mountain. To get out of the sun in a tropical country would be a help once in a while.

Surely there was some reflection of Christ's glory in the natural world around them. A sudden release of such divine beauty as the Transfiguration would likely be manifest in the physical world—a lightness in the air, a sweetness, some sense of loveliness. That is why Peter would exclaim, "It is so nice here. Let us stay awhile. I will build three shelters for you."

How did the three disciples know that the two men with Christ were Moses and Elijah? They must have asked Him later, "And what did you talk about?"

When told they talked of Jerusalem and what was to come there, Peter's face fell. It was ominous. Foreboding. The more so when Christ said, "By the way—we don't talk about this to anyone until I am risen from the dead."

That, too, would puzzle them. What did it mean? They would talk about this later among themselves.

What was the point of this unusual encounter on Mount Tabor if not to prepare the three for the days ahead? The prediction of what was to come on the Son of Man just recently shared with them had only led to Peter's abhorrence of it all, followed by the Lord's severe rebuke, "Get behind Me, Satan!" This remarkable revelation of glory turns out to be a prelude to a dreadful future.

This awesome revelation of His glory in His face, brilliant beyond any bleach, would hopefully deepen their grasp of Who He was and prepare them for the betrayal, for Gethsemani, the arrest and trials, and what followed. Even so, it just sufficed.

If they had been Irish, they would have understood. I mean to say, the Irish seem endowed with a sense of the tragic. Though everything's just fine for now, it won't last. Something is bound to happen that will spoil it. It's waiting its turn in the wings. As an intimate of Kennedy at the scene in Dallas said, "We knew it wouldn't last, but I just didn't think it would come so soon."

It may all be Irish fantasy. Suffering and disappointment touches everyone, after all.

For Christians, it is better to trust in God, no matter how vivid our worry, how real our sense of doom. That's the point of the Transfiguration.

Amen.

WHO DO YOU SAY HE IS?

John 6:1-15

In the late 1920s my father took me to hear William Howard Taft speak at an outdoor political rally. Taft was a former President. My father, who had no special interest in politics, used the speech as an excuse to take a ride in his Model-T Ford. We went a few miles to a large field filled with several thousand people. On the fringe we could scarcely see Taft, let alone hear him. No matter. We were there and we could read his speech in tomorrow's Boston *Post*.

That event, of course, stuck in my mind. How did Jesus ever manage? He often spoke to a single person, to small groups, but just as often to large and very large groups.

Sometimes he spoke on the lakeshore where the smooth surface of the water served as a sounding board, the more so if He was in a boat and somewhat elevated, as church pulpits used to be high, or as we had two elevated platforms in choir for reading the lessons in the Divine Office. Snowmass Abbey had the refectory's Reader perch high up on the wall of the room. Better still, there were natural amphitheaters in the hills, no doubt well-known and used for gatherings. But it still seems a problem to me.

So I got the idea that perhaps with such crowds there was a tactic in use that is never mentioned. The Scriptures make it plausible, for their style lends itself to repeating what was heard.

"A sower went out to sow his seed . . ." And the crowd would repeat, *"A sower went out to sow his seed . . ."*—gradually getting louder and louder as the number hearing it increased. In the end all would be saying it together.

Christ would lift His hand and continue: ***"Some of the seed fell on rocky ground . . ."*** *"Some of the seed fell on rocky ground . . . ,"* etc.

A kind of participatory liturgy. An engaged audience. With increasing interest in seeing how it would turn out, what would follow. Not to say an excellent memory device, for each could tell the story later.

"A man went down from Jerusalem to Jericho . . ." *"A man went down from Jerusalem to Jericho . . ."* Time and time again, until the whole crowd was saying it in unison.

"He fell among robbers who beat him up and left him half dead . . ." *"who left him half dead."*

"And a Levite went down the road and passed him by . . ." *"And a Levite went down the road."*

"And a Pharisee went down the road and passed on the other side . . ." And so on.

"Who has ears to hear, let him hear."

And the classic one—He was a classic story teller. ***"A man had two sons . . ."*** Repeated and repeated.

"The younger son asked for his inheritance and received it." Repeated on and on.

"He went to a far country and blew his fortune in loose living." And they would all laugh, "Typical! Typical!" They are all ears. ***"The money is gone, he got a job taking care of pigs."*** And they would laugh again.

"And the pigs ate better than he did."

Christ would have that whole crowd under his spell.

And so we come to the reading for today (John 6:1-15).

"Have you any bread? Have you fish?"

"Yes. Barley loaves. Two fish."

"Tell them to sit down."

At the back of the crowd they would not know what was going on up front with Jesus. But soon enough someone came by with his robe filled with bread and fish, smoked and salted. He gave the man a half loaf broken off and two fish.

The man says, "Where did you get the bread, the fish?"

And he says, "Jesus."

"And where did Jesus get them?"

"He made them."

"What do you mean, 'He made them?'"

"You heard me. He made them."

And the man slowly eats the bread and the fish, saying over and over to himself, "Who is this man? Who is this man?"

And that is the message I leave with you today: ***Who is this man?***

Amen.

THE DEEPEST OF MYSTERIES

The word seems to have gotten about in short order, I mean the coming of Christ into the world. The more so when one reckons how any word got about in those days. Like a grass fire, the word spread through the Mediterranean world, the Roman world, Paul in Rome, James in Spain, Thomas in India.

Who is this Jesus I hear about? And what is he up to?

Well, He is a prophet, now a carpenter in Galilee, like the prophets of old. He goes about preaching peace and mercy and justice and forgiveness. He heals. He raises the dead. He talks of the Kingdom of God, gives sight to the blind, hearing to the deaf, cleansing to the leper.

And what became of him?

He was put to death by his enemies. He claimed to be the Messiah, the One who is to come. His claim was rejected by Israel.

And that was the end of it?

No way. Three days after His death He rose from the dead. He spent forty days in His resurrected life teaching his disciples.

And then?

And then he returned to his Father, promising to send the Holy Spirit.

This gets even worse. So God was His Father?

Yes, He was the Son of God by His own claim. He was the Second Person of a Trinity. The third was the Holy Spirit whom He and the Father sent after nine days to be with His community, the Church, to guide it to the end of time.

This gets worse and worse. There were then three gods?

No. One God, three Persons. The eternal, the immortal One.

And those who hear Him, follow His teaching, will serve Him here and live with Him hereafter?

Exactly.

You realize this is very wild?

It is indeed.

And the further you go, the wilder it gets.

So? He was born of a virgin, conceived by the Holy Spirit. His presence on earth continues in the sacramental life, especially in the sacrificial Meal, the Sacrifice on the altar, in which His passion, death, and rising are continued in a mystic fashion, the bread and wine becoming the Body and Blood: Presence, Sacrifice for His faithful, until the end of time.

This, in a few words, is the faith that spread through the Mediterranean world, the Greco-Roman world, and continues to do so through all the world. Prayer and study of the story, Old and New codices, led only to deeper conviction. It was all of a piece. It all fit together. And, it all made sense despite of, or perhaps because of, the extravagance of its claims.

The early Church was especially drawn to the mystery of the Trinity. This, the deepest, fundamental, most profound of all Christian truths, captivated the early Christian mind, led to endless study, theories verbalizing the unexplainable, not to say endless dispute, condemnation, heresy, fresh enunciation in creed, the fruit of the councils. To all it was the most absorbing of interests. We are indebted to them, these early theologians, for beautiful doctrines on the most profound truths.

Religion has a passionate attraction for people, and notably the Catholic religion. The story continues, and we are part of it in a very special way. All of which baffles me, intrigues me, overwhelms me, and delights me.

Like the first people who heard of the Christian faith so many centuries ago when Christ first came, we are a deep people, an immortal people, to whom the profound mysteries of our Faith and the deepest meaning serve as the greatest enrichment of our lives. There is no greater happiness than to love God—and it is forever.

Amen.

LIVING THE FAITH

BEGIN IN YOUR OWN HEART

Luke 6:37-49

Today is Quinquagesima Sunday. Fifty days until Easter. According to the same ancient tradition, last week was Sexagesima Sunday, sixty days until Easter, and the Sunday before that was Septuagesima, seventy days until Easter. It follows that next Sunday is Quadragesima Sunday, forty days until Easter, the season of Lent, forty days of fast. The numbers are rounded and thus do not add up, but they are adequate. So, once out of Epiphany and its season, the major celebrations since Advent, we have our eyes set on the Resurrection, or better, on the Passion, Death, and Rising of the Lord, the most significant event in history.

Having your eyes fixed on time's peak event is very healthy. It is healthy for its realistic entry into suffering, that through Christ's Passion and Death, we come to know the Rising of the Lord in victory over sin and death.

Otherwise, how would we cope with the human scene, a scene of worldwide misery of every kind, an unending parade of the tragic. Today. Live. In color.

How we deal with it at all except in relation to the Savior of the world, who entered into suffering and made it redemptive, turned the evil of humankind into an encounter with mercy in his own flesh and blood.

To be sure, in the course of a year we go through Christian history from its ancient roots in Advent through the Nativity and all the events of his life on to the Last Day and the final, closing Judgment. We do it not in a mere historical review, but in a very real, mystical entry into these profound scenes.

Our relationship to the encounter is a great deal more than mere witness as onlookers. We are participants, for our sins are involved. We had a hand in the Passion, and still do. You may think yourself a mere passive viewer, but you are quite mistaken. Your very passive viewing is itself your response to divine events.

As if the yearly encounter with the salvation story is not enough, we have it daily in the Eucharist, for we know the Mass is the Passion, Death, and Rising of the Lord, now being put to death by sinners. "What you do to the least of these you do to me." Christ's Passion, Death and Rising are transcendent events, surpassing time, in the world until it is all over. The last Mass will be offered when the last sin is done. Christ heals this miserable situation by his mercy, calls us to new life, to rise from the dead, to enter into glory.

In the face of such cosmic realities, it seems rather lame to speak of noting the splinter in your brother's eye rather than being aware of your own hampered vision. Is that to be taken as an answer to the world scene?

It seems so, for if the flaw in your brother is a problem with you, does that not indicate a critical view of your own flaws? You cannot treat others any way except the way you treat yourself. If you can be savage in your comments on another, no one need doubt you are just as savage in your own heart, revealed in your speech. The beam in your own eye has never been removed in mercy nor the speck you see in your brother's eye.

We need to meet mercy if we are to do mercy to others. Anything less is sheer waste. The sinful heart that has accepted Christ's mercy approaches another in quite a different mode than does the one foreign to it.

The healing of the world does not begin in some far-off land that we must hasten to help, but in the geography of your own heart. There the sinner is washed in mercy and becomes thereby an instrument of mercy, not merely in his prayers, but in everything he does. He is a vessel of grace. We cannot heal all the world's problems, but we begin with our own heart if our help is to amount to anything.

Our response is not limited to prayer for the afflicted. We practice justice, feed the hungry, clothe the naked, visit the sick, bury the dead. We forgive injury and do not resort to revenge, to reprisal, to contempt. In our world. Where we are.

It costs nothing and is worth more than anyone can tell. It is the way the world is healed, with Christ dying daily everywhere and we with him.

Since the healing process is so slow, as it always is, we need to look ahead to the triumph at the end when Christ, put to death by humankind how many times, rises in glorious mercy. Amen.

CHRIST-LIKE FORGIVENESS

John 8:1-11

Since both parties were to be stoned according to the law, we have in today's story of the adulterous woman but a part of the total picture. One gathers that they were not stoned together in the custom of the times. Some say that the parties were stripped. Whether that be so in today's piece is not said. However, assuming that the prosecuting men were a group, they could more or less encircle the woman out of some sense of decency. But when they came upon Christ by accident, or by God's design, on their way out of the city, they let the woman be seen, "making her stand in front of everybody." Christ felt compassion for her humiliation and quietly found something to do on the ground. He may have been very angry at the group for using her as a ploy against him as much as for their arrogance.

Christ deftly parries their ploy and ignores the issue of the law. He applies it with a new proviso, "Let anyone among you who is without sin be the first to throw a stone at her." They were both stung and stunned. He was a mastermind, a shrewd lawyer, and an astute judge.

They threw her clothes at her and, "beginning with the eldest," as the text says, "they withdrew." Actors to the end, looking good.

These people loved God, upheld his cause, but did so blindly, motivated by a desire to come off well. "Self-righteous" is the proper word, a disease the pious are prone to.

How does one at the same time be pious and not self-righteous? Jesus has your answer: by mercy, the three-tiered mercy, to God, to neighbor, to self.

Forgive God, to begin with. Surely, you have something against God, life being what it is. Have you forgiven Him?

Has your neighbor done nothing against you? Not likely. Have you forgiven him? Sometimes monks do not forgive but carry grudges, resentments, justified umbrage for what someone has done to them: superior, inferior, equal. What nonsense!

And you, my brother, have you forgiven yourself? Alas, this is the last. Here it starts, here it ends, forgiveness is meaningless when it does not start at home, in your own heart. Forgive what you have done, or should have done, or could have done and did not. In the silence of the cloister the voice of the past can haunt you, can point fingers at you, can snicker.

Unless mercy is continued here it is not going to amount to much in terms of others. Charity starts at home. As someone said, "My own heart let me more have pity on."

You're not up to it? That's likely. Well then, pray for the grace to be a person of mercy, for yourself, for others, and toward God. It is not a matter of liking everybody. That's impossible. But to love everyone?—that is possible, and it is what we are called to do.

Love means you don't distinguish your children. You love the gifted one, the happy one, the one less gifted, the awkward one, the troubled one—you love them all, else what kind of father or mother are you? What sort of monk?

You don't know much as a parent or as a monk if you don't know Christ as a man of mercy.

Join the ranks of love. Why are you standing there? Why linger on the fringe, standing in the back, hesitant and fearful?

If you enter the realms of mercy your world changes. For that milieu, from that climate, your attitude is one of Jesus. You don't throw stones, you show compassion.

> Woman, has no one condemned you?
> No one Sir.
> Neither do I condemn you. Go your way.

Forgive God. It is important.
Forgive your neighbor. It is the law.
Forgive yourself. It's Christ-like. Amen.

FORESIGHT

Matthew 25:1-13

When there is a serious lack in your world within, dreams will often come to help. They do so by using material from daily life to make up a scene or two which add up to an effective message. If that does not get through, later another try will be made with the same meaning but using fresh material from yesterday or the day before, spinning some incident with the message said again in a new way.

So Jesus today. The story is that of the ten virgins with lamps attending the wedding rite. Some provident, some not, and with disastrous results for the improvident.

The message is foresight. A beautiful word with a host of partners: forebode, forecast, foreclose, forefather, forego, foreman, forenoon—all dealing with some view of the future in relation to the present.

It is a theme Jesus often returns to: don't build a house unless you have money enough to finish it. Foresight.

When you build the house, take care that the foundation is good lest it collapse in a crisis. Foresight.

Make peace with your enemy on the way to court, lest the court deal severely with you. Foresight.

Don't go into battle unless you are sure your forces are capable of meeting those of your enemy. Foresight.

Don't agree to go along with the Lord unless you are willing to pay the price of discipleship. Foresight.

Jesus uses the matter of the day, today's experience, to point out the need always to have an eye on the future.

Having an eye on the future may seem to take attention from the matter at hand unless you realize that the matter at hand can only be dealt with realistically when you have an eye on the future. A thoughtless plunge into the current situation can be a disastrous ploy.

We are immortal, and to deal with life as if we were not will lead to unhappiness. Nothing gives luster to living as much as having an immortal connection. You cannot deny reality and succeed at it.

We can understand foresight as quite similar to prudence, the first of the cardinal virtues. Foresight has a local ring, while prudence is from the Latin and hence has a special tone. But, we understand prudence, what it means to be a prudent man or a prudent woman. An insurance company is not named Prudential without a point.

Since I brought up the cardinal virtues, the pivotal virtues, they are the hinges on which the doors of our lives swing. *Cardo* in Latin means "hinge." They are the familiar four: prudence, temperance, justice, and fortitude.

Temperance is our familiar Benedictine *ne quid nimis*—nothing to excess. That is a sound principle in monastic life and everyone's life. The happy medium is neither too much nor too little.

Justice is giving to God and to others what is their due.

It would seem to me that fortitude would be a necessary quality today. Trying times, anxious times, troubled times call for a brave spirit rooted in the grace of God. Anyone can be brave when things go well, but to remain steady in hope, trusting in God, carrying on as best we can, is noble indeed. That is for sure when the weather is rough.

Failure, lack of success, obvious weakness, evil forces at work, Godly forces at bay—these must call us to hope in God, to trust in his mercy, to the will to live and to love while there is still a heart in us.

The beginning is foresight, to scan the sea and sky before we launch into the deep. Foresight in daily life is common sense, and it is also common sense in the spiritual life. Where did you come from? What are you here for? Where are you going?

Or, in simple terms, what is it all about? To have answer to such a question is gift indeed, and to respond to that gift is a gift to the world. It is to witness not by talk, not by word, not even by deed, but by being.

Foresight is not only to have oil in your lamps. It is to have light in your heart because your sights are set on Heaven and eternal Glory.

Amen.

THE MASTER KEY

John 12:20-33

Father McKenzie says that there is no Hebrew word for "thunder." They use "voice" instead, which leads to a lot of happy confusion. It would take no great imagination for any of us to think of a voice of God when we hear thunder. That an earlier people did so is no surprise. But it does seem clear that at least on three occasions there was a real voice, not merely thunder, and all were at very significant times in the life of Jesus.

The first at his baptism when, contradicting the view of John, he submitted to a baptism for sinners in order to state clearly that he identified with them, was their agent, their advocate before the Father. His stance was vindicated by the dove of the Spirit and by the voice, "This is my Beloved Son. Hear him." We are off on a significant journey.

Late in his ministry, Jesus was at pains to describe what lay just ahead and, far more clearly and in explicit terms, that he would "go to Jerusalem, suffer greatly from the elders, the chief priests, and the scribes, and be killed and on the third day be raised." To which Peter replied in strong objection, "God forbid, Lord, no such thing can happen to you." Jesus' response was, "Get behind me, Satan." This dreadful episode, so disturbing to the twelve, was followed by the Transfiguration, with Peter, James, and John. "This is my Beloved Son, with whom I am well pleased. Listen to him," said the voice.

Today's episode in John 12 is on the heels of the triumphant entry into Jerusalem, the waving of palms, "Hosanna to the Son of David." When Greeks are brought to Jesus, he is at pains both to welcome them and to make plain to them the essence of his teaching in terms of the Cross. The scene of triumph is followed

73

by a gospel of suffering and death for him and for all who followed him. Then a voice from heaven responds to Jesus' prayer, "Father, glorify Your Name." It said, "I have glorified it and will glorify it again." The crowd then heard it and said it was thunder, but others said it was an angel. "The voice came for your sake," said Jesus. So, it was a voice.

The reconciliation of opposites is so much at the heart of our faith and necessarily at the heart of our response to it. Never retreat from a confrontation with such truth. There is nurture in it, depth, point, purpose, and meaning. The very fact of our immortality is already such a challenge, and yet it is so fundamentally an aspect of our mortality.

A friend is in charge of housing at a large western university. The master key is lost or stolen. In order to avoid disaster, new locks are quietly ordered to be installed at once. There was a need for about six thousand locks. Schlage, the lock company, did not have that many on hand. They provided what they had and said they would have the rest in twenty-four hours. They did. Six thousand locks and one master key. Thousands of locks, all different, yet one key would open them all. So small an instrument could be interpreted in so many ways.

A friend, a student of C. S. Lewis, visited Wheaton College to see the works of Lewis housed there along with the work of several other evangelists. My friend picked up a volume from Lewis's library, *Eternal Life* by Frederick von Hugel. On the inside cover Lewis had written in pencil,

> It is not an abstraction called humanity that is to be saved. It is you yourself—yourself, not another. It is your soul and, in some sense not fully understood, even your body, that was made for the high and holy place. And that you are—your sins excepted—every fold and crease and nook and cranny of your individuality, destined from all eternity to fit God as a glove fits your hand. And that intimate particularity which you can hardly grasp yourself, much less communicate to your fellow creatures, is no mystery to him. He made those ins and outs that he might fill them. He gave you just so curious a life because it is the key designed to unlock the door of all the myriad doors in him.

So far Lewis. How nice! We are all of us so very individual, made in God's image and likeness because we are, we are forever, and we are one. There is only one you and there will never be another.

The key, of course, is the cross. For all our differences, for all our singularity, it is the cross that for one and all is the key that opens the door of his heart. Our specificity is, to be sure, basic, and in our singularity we enter the heart, the life of God. That is possible because Jesus is the master key. The lock turns, the door opens for us, for each, for you, for me, not some great mass of humanity, but for individuals, deeply loved and deep in the heart of God.

Amen.

EVEN THERE, EVEN THEN:
I AM WITH YOU

Luke 9:18-24

This morning's excerpt from the Gospel of Luke is no great favorite. "The Son of Man must undergo great suffering and be rejected by the elders, chief priests, and scribes, and be killed, and on the third day be raised. If any want to become my followers, let them deny themselves and take up their cross daily and follow me. For those who want to save their life will lose it, and those who lose their life for my sake will save it."

There is peace and there is peace. World War II was thought by those engaged in it and those paying for it, a good war, a worthy war—if any war can be worthy. One fought with a good conscience, with peace of heart. Here we have peace and war together. On the contrary, today many feel the present conflict in Iraq is not a worthy one, and so they have no peace of heart, no good conscience on it.

Peace, then, in one sense of the word, means that whatever the situation , there can be peace in the heart. Your conscience is at rest. Christ, then, promises not a life of no conflict, but a heart at peace with itself.

My recent visitors carried tales of distress over the scene in Boston, where the archbishop is closing sixty parishes of a total 357, some with schools. No doubt the archbishop has peace in his heart and acts in good faith, with just concern, even though what he brings about causes anger, resentment, and accusation. He is supported in his peace because the process was long and involved, done with every possible care. Yet, it is certain that such a decision will not be accepted easily. Who wants to close churches? Least of all, who wants his own church closed? One does not need any imagination to see this scene as a very difficult one for almost everyone. Even though the closing of a monastery in France is disappointing to us, thousands of miles away, closing down our own monastery would be a far different story.

Presumably, Christ has such situations in mind when he spoke of his coming not being peaceful. The consequence of your faith, your commitment to it, may suddenly take an unexpected turn, may force a decision you are not happy about, that is going to cost you much.

We all know the beauty of vows, of ordination, and yet the day may come when the vow and the anointing will make extraordinary demands of you; a scene in no way identified as peace. It is war, and real war—the fruit of following Christ, the unexpected sequel to response, the price of peace. How could the disciples have possibly known what was in store for them when he said, "Follow me," and they answered? Their performance revealed their response, often poor.

Yet, it is only in the conflict born of commitment that we know peace. He promises strife and he gives peace.

That is not today's theme song. Such commitment is not selling well at all. Years ago Bishop Sheen preached on contemporary unwillingness to commit one's self to God, to Church, to spouse, to vow. It was nothing new in his day and certainly not in ours. There is little of the sort of peace Christ speaks of.

Or in closing churches, for that matter. Three reasons were given: shifting populations, less Mass attendance, and fewer priests.

With a Catholic population of over two million, Mass attendance on Sundays averages only seventeen percent. One-third of the parishes operate at a loss. The upkeep of parish plants is neglected for want of wherewithal. So, it was a difficult decision in a difficult situation. Christ's answer to that was, do what is to be done, however difficult.

What is to be noted, of course, is that the scene is the result of the faithful's actions. The churches are closed because there are not enough people to keep them open. No parish can survive on seventeen percent participation.

Which point returns us to Christ. The impossible situations we get ourselves into and which require a response in faith are often enough the fruit of our own misdeeds.

Christ says, even there and even then, "I am with you." Whatever you have done, whatever disastrous situation you have gotten yourself into by sin or by foolish behavior or even blindness and mistake, I am with you. I will not leave you. Call to me; I will hear you. It is not I who robbed you of your peace. It is you yourself. And yet, even there, even then, I am with you.

Amen.

MORAL POWER

Luke 19:1-10

Michael Casey, an Australian Cistercian and theologian, writes in his book, *Fully Human, Fully Divine*, an interesting and provocative note. "The creedal statement that Christ is a 'perfect' human being is easily misunderstood. It can make us imagine Jesus as a youthful man with a great body, good teeth, an attractive face. The historical Jesus may have been heavier than we, overweight by our standards, middle-aged and bald."

That the new Eve should have such a son is indeed a bit puzzling, but let that be for now. One thing is sure, the hero in today's Gospel is much like the fancied Jesus in that he was short, not likely very heavy, otherwise he would not be given to climbing sycamores. When Jesus caught sight of him up there, he asked a companion, "Who is that?" A moment's inquiry gave the answer, "It's Zacchaeus." Then, with a touch of disgust, "He's a tax collector." The response of Jesus was instant. He called up to Zacchaeus, "Come down, Zacchaeus! I want to stay with you today."

Why would Jesus do such a thing? He would know, would He not, that no one would have any truck with a tax collector, let alone stay with him, dine with him? Why does he deliberately antagonize people, exasperate them? Is this going to help his mission? He should know that people will be furious, and yet he goes ahead anyway.

He wants to make a point, of course, and make it loud and clear. "I did not come to call the righteous, I came for sinners. How many times must I tell you?"

It is possible in regard to the many journeys of Pope John Paul II that you sense them as goodwill ventures in which he spreads good feelings, praises beautiful cities, and comments on lovely countries and their faithful people. Then he preaches on some aspect of the faith that could be said anywhere at anytime.

I suspect he is in all this more like Jesus than otherwise. I do recall that the Pope had some good points to make, strong ones, when he was among us. He did not find our culture, our style, without flaw, and he said so.

Why I have such a vivid memory of it I do not know, except that I once visited the Philippines and there heard much about the then-ruling Ferdinand Marcos and his wife Imelda. I was astounded when I heard or read the Pope's major address in the presence of Marcos. He was very direct, pointed, and explicit about the disorders in the Marcos regime, and listed them. It was a breathtaking speech. At the end, Marcos discarded his prepared speech and made a few general remarks about improving the situation. But what was clear, and both he and the people seemed to know it, was that he was finished. The Pope's listeners suddenly sensed what they were putting up with, and there was no need to do so. It was a moment of enlightenment.

Not long after there followed the "People Power" revolution, an uprising and ouster of Marcos and his wife who took refuge in Hawaii before it was too late. It was a revolution without gunfire, without violence, choreographed by the Cardinal of Manila. It was a most remarkable achievement, a new kind of warfare.

We know, of course, that the same sort of peaceful, non-violent uprising toppled the communists in Poland. It was, once again, a new kind of warfare, a movement of moral power. It makes the current scene in Iraq look so archaic, so outmoded, so dated. Violence is no longer the accepted tactic for achieving good ends. There is a spiritual power in people that is stronger than weaponry.

It is, of course, rooted in truth. The Pope spoke the truth without rancor, without anger or heavy emotion, but simply, honestly, and forcefully. The moral impact was enormous.

I suppose you could say, in a sense, that when John Paul went to Manila, he went to the worst sinner of all and revealed his sins to him in such a way that there was no refuge except in admission and repentance. That is why Marcos went to Hawaii, not only because he had to, but also because he wanted to. He died there some time later.

I need not point out to you the significance of a life of honest confrontation of evil within the human heart, exposing it to the power of God's grace, both for yourself and for the world. The warfare is within and it is nonviolent. It is victorious in Christ. Stick with it. What you look like does not matter that much.

Amen.

"DO YOU LOVE ME?"

John 21:1-19

This morning's Gospel selection is surely one of the loveliest. It seems much a carefully programmed farewell gathering that Jesus worked out—a last time together by the lake. At least for some of them.

The elements are clear:

> A night of fruitless fishing by his disciples.
> A miraculous catch at the suggestion of the figure on the
>   beach.
> The encounter with Jesus, with first recognition by John, of
>   course.
> The breakfast he has prepared—the fire and the bread and
>   the fish.
> Their sharing in the breakfast with part of the fish-catch.
> The meal together on the shore.
> And the dialog with Peter.

What a beautiful morning! What a touching adieu! Christ comes onto a scene of human failure, no fish, a night's work for nothing.

His response to that is abundant harvest.

This will be their life's story in the years to come:

> failure and success
> darkness and light
> evil and good.

No matter what the scene, Christ will be there.

They gather in a meal, take food together. This too will be their life's story:

the food of God's work, God's grace, to be shared with one another and with all the world, community and church.

We, too, are characterized by a gathering together to take food, human and divine. The ritual of the altar is as beautiful as the ritual of the table, the liturgy of the Eucharist, the liturgy of the refectory, in the community, in the Church.

Then the dialogue of Jesus and Peter on the heart of the matter, that is to say, love.

The incident is as beautiful as anything in Scripture, on the shores of time and eternity. The basic question, "Do you love me?"

This is a qualified love. "Do you love me more than these? If you are my chosen one, is your love correspondingly greater?"

To move it beyond sentiment, beyond feeling and pious emotions, Jesus asks him three times, "Do you love me?"

Peter was surely near tears, yet the Lord did not spare his feelings. Peter had to learn. He must acknowledge that self-reliance is no reliance at all. Posturing and performance are meaningless. In a crisis Peter was a disaster. He admitted it but was absolved by a look from Jesus. He had best not forget it and never rely again on human prowess. In three questions on love, Christ undoes the three denials.

Find your place at this farewell and answer the invitation after failure and fruitless endeavor, to try again on the other side. Share the fruit of it with Jesus himself and his followers. Pledge your love, rooted in grace, aware of weakness and mindful of failure. But do it in joy. One cannot be morbidly timid for lack of courage or dismal experience. Rather, be confident and trusting and in good cheer.

Sooner or later we will meet him on the shore. Indeed, perhaps we have already done so many times, usually after failure. There we will meet refreshment and renewal and a challenging encounter and a call to love.

Amen.

LIGHT OF THE WORLD,
SALT OF THE EARTH

Mark 9:49-50
2 Kings 2:20

Last week we all carried a candle in procession. It was a lovely scene. Candles, totally utilitarian centuries ago, have become almost wholly aesthetic. A burning candle says so much. It can give another tone to an otherwise traditional dinner. Candles burn at Mass and give light of another kind. We use candles in so many liturgical ways. These are not ordinary candles from petroleum, but sweet-scented candles from the wax of the bees' honeycomb, at least a good percentage of it, enough that anyone can notice. I once attended a function at Soldiers' Field in Chicago in 1954 in honor of Our Lady. The last gesture was for all to light their candles in the evening shadows. It was splendid! There were thousands of candles.

This week we receive the ashes of Lent, quite another scene. The one and only time ashes function in a liturgical rite and carry a powerful message in a monastery ritual. No other appearances do ashes make. The move toward cremation does bring a new note to our common prayer and gives a new impact to the single prayer "*Memento homo*," "Remember, man that you are dust and to dust you will return."

Today's Gospel tells of another use of material things to speak a spiritual message. "For everyone will be salted with fire. Salt is good, but if salt has lost its saltiness, how can you season it? Have salt in yourselves and be at peace with one another."

In today's reading Jesus says, "You are the salt of the earth. But what if salt goes flat? How can you restore its flavor? Then it is good for nothing but to be thrown out and trampled underfoot."

Salt makes a perfect symbol precisely because it is hard to define its message. One needs insight, an intuitive grasp, a poetic imagination to read salt right.

Salt used to be a required part of the baptismal rite, except in an emergency. I understand that today it is optional.

In the blessing of the water before Mass there is a prayer of blessing of salt and the adding of a bit of salt to the blessed water. This, too, is now optional.

Since salt at baptism is hardly worth speaking for in our context, salt in the blessing of the water each Sunday and a bit of it added to the water is another matter. I am going to suggest it to the proper people that we consider this feature.

The reason is clear. The use of salt is gone in the liturgy when the two options are acted on negatively. That would seem a pity, for Christ's reference to salt is then rendered archaic and out of touch. The use of salt, even in so modest a manner, makes real the reference to salt that Christ uses. God knows we use lots of salt, but giving it expression also in the liturgy connects its use to Christ's use for us, and so enlarges the sayings. If the exact meaning of Christ's words about salt are not quite clear, so much the better. When things are too obvious the charm is wanting. Water is indeed a great symbol, but its meaning is so obvious that it is less powerful.

The real issue, of course, is seeing the whole world and all of creation as somehow sacramental. Using various items in the created world in our prayer life reminds us of that. Bread and wine, water, oil, candles, incense, salt, and ashes come to mind. Yet they are but the beginning. We also use bells, flowers, music, vesture, gesture, art and architecture, space and silence, darkness and light, the touch, the anointing, the embrace. Some of them are rare, like prostration for vows and ordinations. Some of them are common, like the bow and the sign of the cross. All of them mingle earth and heaven, matter and spirit.

Jesus was rubbed with salt when he was born, for whatever reason. He is indeed the salt of the earth, as are you.

Salt saves as in salted beef, salt pork, salt codfish. Salt preserves in pickles or cabbage. Salt gives savor as in a flat soup, an insipid boiled potato, or a fried egg. Leviticus 2 reminds us, "with all your offerings you shall offer salt."

> "They said to Elisha, 'The water is bad and the land is unfruitful.' He said, 'Bring me a new bowl and put salt in it.' So they brought it to him. Then he went to the spring of water, threw salt in it and said, 'Thus says the Lord, I have made this water wholesome.' So the water has become wholesome, as it is today, according to the word Elisha spoke."

Come, Elisha! Freshen our lives with a touch of your salt. Amen.

VISIONS OF THE REAL AND THE UNREAL

Matthew 9:36–10:9

These past ten days or so I have been having visitations, two of them. The one was a visitation of sickness, some infection that made me miserable and for which the healing medicine made me feel ever so much worse. For this powerful drug was seemingly hallucinogenic and filled my days and nights with visions and nightmares and hallucinations which were so real they left me in no doubt of their reality.

I said to Brother Jude, with a map of Illinois in my hand, "Where was that chicken farm you took me to last night?" He said, matter-of-factly, "There was no chicken farm. You never left your bed." "And the hotel lobby we stayed in until the traffic thinned out?" "There was no hotel lobby." I was astounded, and that was only one item.

In a few days the visions ended. By then the second visitation was at hand, an archbishop from Madang in New Guinea. In 1982 he made a retreat at my hermitage before being made bishop, and I was at the outdoor ceremony on my way home. Now he begins his visit with a retreat first of all at this abbey. Then he goes to the Divine Word Society's headquarters near Chicago, and then on to Rome and an *ad lumina* visit with the Holy Father and his fellow bishops of New Guinea—all twenty-five of them. Then he moves on to Poland, his home, and to Bonn, Germany, for the papal World Youth Festival.

Of my encounter with the world of visions and fantasy, even some taste of a drugged world, it is in a way what we do in daily life. What we try to do is to relate to the world around us, the world we experience as perhaps genuine.

If the world of imagination is one encounter, so is our encounter with the world we live in: a weighting, a testing, a trying. Good and evil, success and failure, sunshine and darkness are aspects of a world in which we all live. Sorting them out, coping with them, dealing with them are serious dimensions of our lives. Only in the light of the gospel, the grace of God, the Spirit given us in Christ can we attain the wisdom that keeps us neither remote from reality, lest we see what is there, nor overwhelmed by it and so submerged in darkness. How tempting it is to see the Church perfect, and how tempting also to see the Church a disaster. Neither version is near the truth. Only divine wisdom can provide the light of faith to see the whole picture, the total scene.

If my efforts to understand what was going on in my mind could finally lead me to a proper understanding of it all, so in faith we can see the Church whole—at once both human and divine, full of human foibles, yet rich in God's grace and power.

So the archbishop would come by each day for an hour and talk of things, things good and things not so good, signs of hope and signs of discouragement and failure. It is an honest vision made honest by the grace of God and the light of the Holy Spirit.

Giving up on the Church is nothing new. For many that is the answer to their experience. Yet, no experience, good or bad, is complete without the vision of grace. To complete the vision in grace is our business and our function.

The twenty-five bishops of Papua New Guinea, who met with Pope Benedict, carried to him good news and bad. At the feet of Peter they heard encouraging words about the beauty of what they do.

The nightmare born of drugs is a perfect picture of the hopeless mind barren of grace. The light of grace enables us to see what is real and what is not, in your life and mine, in the life of the church.

"Then Jesus summoned the twelve disciples and gave them authority over unclean spirits, to cast them out and to cure every disease and every sickness."

Amen.

A GOD OF MERCY

John 20:19-31

This is Divine Mercy Sunday, declared such by Pope John Paul II, April 30, 2000. I offer a few thoughts on three people who were connected with the city of Cracow in Poland. The three are John Paul II, Sister Marie Faustina Kowalska, and Rudolph Hoess. They were not precisely contemporaries, but people of our time.

John Paul, Karol Wojtila, was made bishop of Cracow in 1936, a cardinal in 1967, and Pope in 1978. Sister Faustina died in 1938, a sister of Our Lady of Mercy. Rudolph Hoess was executed at Auschwitz in 1947.

It was the Archbishop of Cracow, Karol Wojtila, who asked one of his local theologians to do a critical analysis of the writings of the sister. Father Ignatius Rozycki was unwilling to do so because for many years he had deep suspicions about her reputed sanctity, above all with the revelations attributed to her. He thought her a simple woman, very pious, the victim of hallucinations with an undercurrent of hysteria, the heroism of her life a lost cause. So, he wanted no part in the proceedings begun by the Archbishop.

Later, out of simple curiosity, he began to read the diaries about which he had so much negative opinion and ended up being converted by them to a new view of the nun. He spent ten years in an exhaustive study and produced a strictly scientific work published after her death in 1983.

The sister's writings had been condemned by the Vatican in 1958, a decision instigated by John XXIII in 1959, and the prohibition declared no longer binding in 1978. She was beatified in 1992 by Pope John Paul and canonized in the year 2000. On the latter occasion he declared the Sunday after Easter "Divine Mercy Sunday."

In the prison in Cracow was confined Rudolph Hoess, the Nazi in charge of the Auschwitz concentration camp and directly responsible for the deaths of three million Jews. He was tried at Nuremberg and Warsaw, confessed, and was condemned to death.

While in solitary confinement at Cracow he heard the bell of the local Carmel. That began a return to the faith of his childhood and the whole process of healing and forgiveness.

He eventually asked for a priest, and a priest was found, Father Ladislaw Lohn, S.J., provincial of the Jesuit southern province of Poland. He went to the convent where Sister Faustina had lived and asked all the sisters to pray earnestly while he went to the prison to hear the confession of Hoess. It took two hours. Hoess was reconciled with the Church, made his confession, and the next day received Holy Communion with tears in his eyes. He then wrote to his wife and five children, expressed sorrow for his crimes, and begged forgiveness of the people of Poland. He was executed on April 16, 1947.

You no doubt have heard this remarkable story. I used to tell it frequently in the retreat house. As might be expected, the response was not universally positive. Some were not impressed. Some said he should go to Hell and deserved to.

My response was not only an emphasis on the reality of God's mercy but also the teaching on Purgatory. I would say, "You know he could be, and gladly so, in Purgatory until the end of time. But in the end, he will be saved. He will be saved."

We are sinners all. We are indebted to that Mercy. We thank God that we have not done worse, are grateful for His solicitude.

I am not sure how much status mercy has in capitalist society, whether it is always mentioned in one's resume. I am sometimes disturbed by the glee expressed by families who have been victims of tragedy, how they witness the perpetrator of the crime condemned to death or life imprisonment. Let that pass.

Monks and nuns, not to say Christians, are to be a people of mercy. They are familiar with the works of mercy, spiritual and corporal.

Pray for the living and bury the dead.

God of Mercy, be merciful to us all. Amen.

THE MASS

THE GREATEST OF THE SACRAMENTS

John 13:1-15

The end room on the first floor of the retreat house was often occupied, in time gone by, by a permanent guest. I am not recommending this. I am just bragging on it.

Everett Edelen of a fine, old family was a good example. He was living a wretched life, and we offered him hospitality and the hope of a better life. He accepted and was healed. He became a real Christian. He was robbed of the four thousand dollars everyone knew he kept in his watch pocket and was badly beaten up at the gate when he came back late one night. He was not dearly loved in the area.

Then there was Leo Gannon, for years the retreat house resident secretary. We bought him a house in Louisville when he retired, but when widowed, he wanted to spend his last days here. He did.

Or Bernard Fox, retired, who became our driver and took the monks where they needed to go. He began the practice of having fresh fruit always at table.

Dr. Dan Walsh had been a Columbia professor and later a priest in Louisville. He lived with us for a time. Then he lectured here and locally. There were others, many others.

Monks preach hospitality and practice it. Years ago, about a century, give or take a few years, the third floor east had private rooms reserved for priests who had drinking problems. Bishops would send them here for penance and reform for a month or two or longer. To be sure, we did nothing special for them in terms of their addiction. No one did in those days. Alcohol was thought a moral problem. Carl Jung, the Oxford group, Alcoholics Anonymous from Akron, proved otherwise and developed a program that combined the grace of God—the moral side—and good psychology—the praxis side. The Servants of the Paraclete developed the first Catholic treatment center in Jemez Springs, New Mexico, in 1947.

Today we have another problem—thought moral—and not restricted to priests any more than alcohol is. Not a great deal is known about it. At last we are beginning to learn that the grace of God and sound psychology are involved.

Kindness, mercy, compassion, and healing hospitality are all in order. All are monastic values and practices, rooted in the Gospel, expressed in washing one another's feet. Yet it all must be intelligent and effective, not mere ritual or simplistic "dogoodism." We learn. We try. God knows we try.

We celebrate today one of the greatest events in history. We can list the three after creation itself: the Incarnation of Christ; the Passion, Death, and Rising of Christ; and, tonight, the Eucharist. And after the service of the Eucharist: the priesthood. You understand properly, I think, if you see the Eucharist combining the other two major events: the incarnation and the passion, death, and rising.

The Eucharist is Christ incarnate. It is the passion, death, and rising of Christ. It is Christ in another mode, another form or manner, the human Christ, the divine Christ, the Body and Blood, soul and divinity of Christ—but in a new way, under the form of a meal, of food and drink, of bread and wine. Here, too, passion, death, and rising, in a new form.

That is why Eucharist is sacrifice, presence, food, and drink. It is the greatest of the sacraments, the most profound. The priesthood, begun this day, carries it out. He is the priest who stands at the altar as Christ and offers the sacrifice as Christ. The bread and wine, having become the sacrificial Christ, is put to death by sinners. By you. By me. By all. Timeless. Out of time, yet in time.

Every moment of the day and night, Christ is offered to the Father for the sins of humankind. He pleads for mercy, for pardon, for healing. The pledge of that, the promise of it, is in the Communion in which the Body and Blood of the saving victim is received.

There is, of course, nothing like it in the world. It is simple enough for a child to grasp, deep enough for the most gifted mind, challenging the most noble heart, the deepest faith.

Since it is the passion, death, and rising, it is also the descent into Hell, in dated language, or, more appropriately, to the regions of the dead to gather those who never knew him on earth, yet who followed the light they had as best they could, the light that is given everyone come into this world.

Granted, a zeal for the faith has carried it to every corner of the world. Granted that untold millions have never heard of Christ. "Lord, what about him?" Peter asked concerning John. The question is more pointed for our failing to carry Christ everywhere. "If it is my will that he remain until I come, what is that to you? Follow me!"

Meanwhile, we practice hospitality, not the hospitality of a good business, but the hospitality of the heart, extended to all who show up at our door, who knock at the gate.

God spare us the day when we would be known as a cheese plant, a bakery, a candy kitchen, a retreat house, and not as a monastery.

The mystery of faith goes beyond obvious hospitality to any comer but extends to all who live, indeed to all the dead Christ visits in each Mass, "that every knee should bow, in heaven, on earth, and under the earth."

I need not remind you, need I, that a people endowed with the gift of faith, totally undeserved, surely not merited, ought in it to expedite the work of Jesus through a life for the salvation of all. That's what He came for. That's what we're involved with. Today. Every day. Really? Really.

Amen.

THE NAME OF THE GAME

Luke 15:1-32

We did not expect the Bourbon Festival in nearby Bardstown, Kentucky, to close down in view of the terrorist attacks on the World Trade Center and the Pentagon. After all, such a festival is a rather silly affair, of no great depth. Even so, it might have made a gesture.

On the other hand, big-time sports is another matter. We were much moved, though also surprised, into a better grasp of the impact of the scene on the East Coast when games were canceled nationwide, professional and collegiate. Games, after all, competitive sport, are the acting out in a harmless way the inner contest in which we all engage, the contest of good and evil. There is good in us and there is evil in us. This is given. The good life is the pursuit of good and the rejection of evil. A game acts it out, and big-time games do it in an impressive way, a spectacular way. The acting out helps us to understand better what we are about, even if not on a conscious level. This is why sport is so attractive and has such a vast number of spectators. It involves actors, players who are highly skilled, often superbly compensated. All is done in a magnificent setting. This is serious business.

We are disturbed when the games end in violence, when hooligans turn rugby into physical, violent encounters. Play is ruined, games become travesty, a sort of lay sacrilege.

So much the worse when evil erupts on our world in a very vicious, powerful way. We are taken aback. Deliberate evil is at work and disturbs us enormously. None of us is immune to evil. We are all aware of its potential within us. To see the struggle carried out by way of a game is one thing. To see actual evil is something else. Hence the need for a pause, for a moment to reflect.

As Christians we move in the sacrifice of the altar beyond the world of play, of games, of contests, into the real world of actual conflict of good and evil on the cross, when humankind reached the depths of iniquity and put the Son of God to death. This continues through time on the human scene. The immolation of Christ is atonement, mercy, and healing. It calls for an admission of sin, an act of sorrow, the reception of pardon and peace. The healing encounter with Christ is communion. This is the answer to the trend to violence in ourselves, in others.

Violence met with violence is not healing, but vindictive. We would do well to pray for mercy, for the afflicting and afflicted. We would do well to pray for mercy, for pity, pardon, and peace in Jesus.

Amen.

CLIMBING THE TREE

Luke 19:1-10

Somewhere at this moment the sun is rising, and somewhere at this moment the sun is setting. Indeed, every moment of the day and the night the sun is rising and the sun is setting. Or it is at high noon or at midnight, somewhere at zenith on the other side of the world. At any moment, of course, all of these events take place somewhere in an unending procession of natural events. Always, somewhere. To be sure, we seldom think of it, yet as a natural phenomenon it is remarkable. One wonders on it.

Today Zacchaeus climbs a tree that he might better see the Lord. Small of stature, he could have elbowed his way through a crowd to be at the front, but he did not. Instead, he ran ahead and climbed a tree and, thus perched, waited for the Messiah to pass in full view. One wonders on it.

"Knock on wood," the folk dictum has it. Or better, "Touch wood." Why? Initially, I assume, because wood is the cross of our salvation. To touch wood is to recall it, to call on it. Or, as a retreatant suggested to me, "For your back, lean against a tree for a while." Healing.

Zacchaeus climbs a tree, and that is significant because on a tree we were redeemed. Zacchaeus was. He not only saw the Lord, he had Him as guest at his table. The sequel was healing. "I'm going to give half of what I own to the poor."

The cross is our salvation, the salvation of the world. What happens on the cross still happens, and all that followed: passion, death, rising, and the sending of the Spirit.

It happens every moment of the day and night. Somewhere Christ is dying and rising for us. As far as I can reckon, from the *Statisticum* from Rome, there is only one country in the world where the Catholic presence is nil, and that is Afghanistan. Even Nepal, that tolerates no foreign religion, has a Catholic presence in works of mercy. The Sisters of Nazareth are there, but not to evangelize. So, even Afghanistan is now no longer without the passion, death, and rising of the Lord since the military chaplains in this terrible situation bring the sacrifice of the Mass to an afflicted land hostile to it.

This sacrifice is no memorial service calling to mind a stupendous event of the past. It is that and much more. The sacrifice is real because the death is real, and the death is real because the sins are real. Not yesterday's sins. Today's. Ours. The world's. This sacrifice is continually offered in the world. Somewhere. Every hour of the day and night.

If the work of the sun is for us a continuous sequel of unbelievable meaning, how then can we not move above a scene of natural, physical events to another plane, the world of faith? We can do so, and do.

"What you do to the least you do to me." The sins we commit against one another are sins against God and his Christ. That is acted out, played out, revealed in the mystery of priest, altar, and sacrifice in which Christ is done to death and rises glorious in prayer to God for mercy, for pardon, for healing. God is with us in our misery.

As the encounter of Zacchaeus from the tree led to the table, so does our encounter with mercy on the cross lead to the table of communion with Christ for our salvation. There, we receive the grace of response to God's love in prayer, in service to others, for the world. Our humble lives take on great beauty because they are lived in union with Christ in prayer for pardon and peace, mercy and healing.

These are not mere gestures made in the right direction but matters of enormous meaning for ourselves and the world. We live and die in union with Christ. By that union our ordinary days and our ordinary nights, our modest lives and unexceptional deaths share in the dream of Christ, the salvation of the world. This is going on all the time, everywhere. It is the hidden meaning of the world.

Zacchaeus climbed more than a tree. It was an act of impulse born of curiosity that led into the heart of the world's meaning.

The universe opened up for him in a simple action no greater than clambering up a sycamore.

There is for sure a sunrise every moment of the day and night. Another Mass is offered, one more rite, same as yesterday and the day before. The world goes on in its madness, oblivious, unheeding.

Well, not everywhere, not by everyone. Some are not mindless who witness the madness. A people of faith can stand almost mute before unfathomable love.

"Come down, Zacchaeus! I will dine with you." The man hastily came down and, later, saw his guest raised on another tree. That tree is raised everywhere in the world and on it hangs our salvation and the salvation of the world. Without it we would have long since perished as we deserve. Praised be the God of mercy.

Amen.

ACTING OUT VICARIOUS GUILT

Matthew 4:1-11

Many years ago, so many, in fact, that it seems in a previous incarnation, I was called home from a mission assignment in the Pacific to do some other work. I returned by way of Europe—as close a route as any other—and so got a look at a few other countries. I do not remember much, but I do remember that Europe was clean, some lands immaculate.

I thought of that last week when I went to see two doctors, one in Lebanon, one in Campbellsville. Their names were fitting enough for a monk's care: Dr. Kirk and Dr. Angel. The roads over one way and back another were unsightly with litter, lots of litter, scattered along the wayside.

Why do Americans do this? They did not bring it with them from Europe, and most of them are ultimately from Europe. Why do they do it here? Foreign visitors are appalled. It is an ugly trait, unsightly, selfish, arrogant, thoughtless. Despite years of effort to eradicate this vice, small progress has been made. Why do they dump trash in our front yard? They don't do it at home. Americans have a lot of good qualities, but this is not one of them. It is disgraceful. People decent enough open the window, throw out the debris, and move on down the road.

So we were thinking about this, another monk and I. What is going on here? I suggest it is rooted in guilt.

Americans are a favored people. They live in one of the richest, best developed, most beautiful countries in the world. Who would argue with that? Further, they are daily exposed to how the rest of the world lives, and that in vivid and dramatic terms. It is absurd to suggest that has no impact. Famine, disease, poverty, ignorance, tyranny, oppression are common. The lot of most.

We live in Paradise. Why? What is so special about us? Nothing, really. Just happenstance. Providence, fortune, good luck.

A person can feel guilty about it in some unconscious way. We know in our hearts that we are not as deserving as we would like to think. So we act out our guilt. We do something nasty. Everyone knows that throwing your trash on the roadside is nasty, and that makes you feel better. I am not special. I am just a sinner and a slob in paradise.

But guilt is not resolved by acting out evil. When a child gives in to an impulse and, instead of being its usual self does something mean, we correct the child. That's not how you deal with evil impulse. You confess it. You acknowledge it. You ask mercy and forgiveness, but you do not act on it. Otherwise, we simply confirm ourselves in evil.

Granted, litter is not a major moral problem, but it is a highly significant one, and one well worth considering during Lent.

If confession is extraordinarily healthy for moral growth, the Eucharist is even more so. In the Eucharist we are confronted with the fruit of evil. The Mass is not mere ritual reenactment of the Passion and Death of the Lord. Ritual reenactment it is, but it is also reality. It *is* the death of the Lord.

That is why the leader is a priest, and why he stands at an altar. He is offering a sacrifice of Christ, and this Christ is put to death by sinners. We are all sinners, you and I. So in the truest sense we witness the consequence of our evil. Our evil put the Son of God to death.

His death, thankfully, becomes merciful pardon and healing. We are forgiven by the Lord we crucified and invited to his table to be united with him in his body and blood, soul and divinity. Then we are bidden to go home and live in love. No need now to act out the evil in us. We have already done so, and in his merciful grace we can live in love.

Here is the healing of guilt. We are sinners healed by the mercy of God. There is no need now to come to terms with guilt by acting on it. We both resist evil and receive pardon. Guilt is overwhelmed by the mercy of God.

It is not enough to dismiss as trifling a care for roadside debris. Such care is, could be, should be, rooted in reverent love for God's death. Thanks be to God for the ecumenical movement, for here is something on which we can all agree. All the religions of the world revere the world as the handiwork of God. Calling on that, activating that, implementing that will be the road to healing, through the love of God and love for God's creation.

We can dismiss all foolish talk of "Mother Nature." Nonsense! There is no Mother Nature. It is God who created the world. Mother Nature is a fantasy. God almighty made the world, and we live in it as God's creatures. We are created to treat it with love and reverence, out of love of God.

Amen.

THE CURTAIN

John 3:14-21

We used to have a purple curtain, floor to ceiling, that marked off the sanctuary for the Lenten season. It was not a total blockout, for the curtain was made of very thin material. It was opened for the consecration in the Mass.

The tradition was still around in the veiling of crucifixes and statues in purple during Lent. A last vestige remains in the veiled cross of Good Friday, and even that is optional.

The idea, of course, was sin. Sin darkens vision, the vision of God, of faith. It erects a barrier between us and heaven, God, the angels and saints. Penitence removes that.

It was also to cultivate reverence and awe for holy things, the cult of the secret. Eastern churches often use an icon screen, back of which the liturgical action takes place. In great cathedrals of the past the high altar was not necessarily visible to all. The choir stalls were in front of it; sometimes a rood screen or other piece blocked the view. Lesson and Gospel were chanted and could be heard. The canon was silent. A bell rung at offertory, sanctus, consecration, and communion made known where the action was at any moment.

Matters are quite otherwise today. All is open, visible, and intelligible. Like Jesus on the cross, the priest faces us and prays in our tongue.

We need no purple curtain to remind us that sin interrupts converse with God. The world around us is a message clear enough. We do not need a litany of the woes of our dreadful time. We see sin and the fruits of it. We come from that same world and carry it with us in our hearts, where we cope with all against evil and live love.

I wrote the Louisville *Courier-Journal* yesterday suggesting that they reprint a page they did a couple of years ago that consisted of photos and brief data on Kentucky's thirty-nine prisoners on Death Row in Eddyville. I suggested that they print it on Good Friday without any comment.

I don't think comment is called for. Putting people to death for a punishment or as a lesson to society is a travesty of justice and an outrage too gross to stomach. That mistakes are made proves it.

Governor George W. Bush, in his years as Texas governor, signed death warrants for 122 and is proud of it. Even in the case of a paranoid schizophrenic with personal pleas from Pope John Paul II and a signed petition for mercy from heads of state in Europe, he went ahead.

This is a nation with one of the highest murder rates in the world and one of the highest prison populations. We are a nation of violence and ugly greed, starving children, and hordes of homeless. Who needs a Lenten curtain?

So Christ comes to be put to death in his people. Passion goes on. "What you do to the least, you do to me." This is not poetic fancy. Thomas Merton's poem about the death of his brother in World War II expresses it: "For in the wreckage of your April Christ lies slain, and Christ weeps in the ruins of my spring."

We know that the Mass is not a mere ceremonial recall of a 2000-year-old event but a living sacrifice of death in every sense of the word. Christ continues to be put to death and he makes of that death a cry of mercy to his Father of forgiveness to those who so sinned.

The last Mass will be offered when the last crime is committed, when no hand is raised against others, no violence done in thought or word or deed, no love betrayed. Then the end will come.

Our response to all this is not condemnation or accusation. We each have a heart, and the human heart is a mysterious amalgam of good and evil which only God and grace can heal. That is the business we are about, to heal the human heart, starting with our own.

Purple is blue with a lot of red. Today (Laetare Sunday), traditionally, priests can wear rose vestments. Rose is purple carried far into red, more blood in a sense, more warmth, more love. That should characterize the heart that looks out on this world with Jesus on the cross, he who said, "If I be lifted up, I will draw all to myself," in mercy and pardon, in grace and peace.

Amen.

MARY

THE NEW EVE

Luke 1:39-56

The fan coil unit in my office in the retreat house is basically a long copper tube weaving back and forth in a grid. In winter, hot water flows through it and in summer cold water. A fan blows over the coil and so sends hot or cold air into the room in season. Fine. But the tube is clogged, and only a trickle of hot water or cold water flows through it, and the room is neither adequately heated nor cooled. Well, they are working on it.

The Church is a pure stream of flowing water carrying the full story of our redemption: entire, authentic, trustworthy. When some left the body of the Church centuries ago to go their own way, they were dependent on their own experience to provide the flowing waters of the faith. Alas, it is a stream clogged with human opinion and private understanding.

This is not said to fault, to condemn, or to put down. Rather, it is said with much sadness. That sadness becomes very great on a day like today when it comes to the Mother of God. So much of the world is deprived of the full story. There is warmth and cool coming through, but it is inadequate.

What a pity not to be comforted with the full story of the Mother of Christ. This is no one's fault, for today's world is the product of yesterday. These poorly served people are no more responsible for their situation than we are for ours. We have been blessed through no merit of our own with the full flow of the message. We had no more to do with that than they had to do with their situation. Surely we can share what we have with prayer.

The Mother of Christ is the Mother of all, and surely the Mother of all Christians. She is present to them as she is to us, loves them as she loves us, and she grieves that they do not love her as they could. No Hail Mary, no Salve Regina, no Madonna, no Blessed Virgin Mary icon, no Rosary, no Lady of Lourdes, no Lady of Guadalupe, no Litany of Loretto, and no Marian Shrine. No pilgrimage to her holy places. No May procession. No Immaculate Conception and no Assumption. How sad. How very sad.

I have led many to the Rosary. It is not that they do not love her. It is more that they don't know her that well, are not on familiar terms with her, do not often pray to her.

I think our devotion to the Mother of God ought to be ecumenical, with a mind to all people, to all the world. This is not mere gesture and pious turn of phrase, but a spirit that moves mountains. Surely it can help remove the barriers that impede the flow of the full story.

What a pity not to see in her the first fruit of the Passion, Death, and Rising of Christ. She is the new Eve, and if she is the new Eve, she is the mother of all living.

Today we celebrate the Assumption, the companion piece to the Immaculate Conception. The start of the story and its end. She is without sin as we were all meant to be, conceived in a human act of love that was not tainted with the original sin of Adam and Eve. Conceived as we all were meant to be in the providence of God but spoiled for the human family by an act of genuine freedom. Since we are one family, we share in the fall.

But she, through her son, was preserved from that in view of her destiny as the Mother of Christ. This was an act of delicate love that would not permit us to be shamed by the birth of a Christ not wholly and perfectly beautiful.

If in her conception she was God's grace at work, so too in her assumption into heaven. Earthly life done, she went to heaven as we are all meant to do. Alas, death intervened, a result of sin.

Christ's victory over sin and death was made evident, visible, effective, first of all in her that we might see in her the magnificence of Christ's victory, a victory we will share in at the last day in our own assumption when death will finally and forever be overcome. In her we see the full fruit of the redemption achieved, the first victory of Christ for us all. We see in her our original mother, Eve, restored to her pristine glory.

The excelling beauty of the poetry of God is nowhere more beautifully written than in her. What a joy for humankind. How sad that all do not know, or know perhaps only partially and not quite adequately.

Thus, a so-called patriarchal Church is also very feminine. Since faith is expressed in prayer and revealed in action, it is no wonder that nobody on earth has done more for women and carries on today, often alone, in a world that trivializes sex, perverts marriage, and puts life to death in a new barbarism.

I suggest that you be grateful for what you have and, like anyone highly favored by God's gifts, be generous in your prayer that all may know what we know and may share in it. Your joy can only be the greater for so doing.

Amen.

BOTH DARKNESS AND LIGHT

Mark 10:2-16

Vernon Robertson, deceased, was an Anglican priest who was very Catholic and who much wanted to be officially and wholly Catholic, but who had some misgivings about what he found to be excessive in Catholic piety in relation to Our Lady. The style was too southern, too Latin, for someone of English background. This grieved him, for he did not wish to become Catholic with that, as it were, stuck in his throat.

He used to travel a lot and was at one time in Chartres Cathedral wandering around looking at things. He walked into an empty chapel where there was but a statue of the Virgin Mary, *la vierge enceinte*, Our Lady with Child. He stood before it, considering it, dwelling on it. "So here is Mary. She has a child within. The child is the Christ, the son of God. Christ is God. She is his mother, the mother of God. So what is all the fuss about?"

In that moment all of his anxiety vanished, and he was at peace. He went on to study at the Beda, was ordained in his class by Pope Paul VI in the Sistine Chapel, went on home to the Diocese of Louisville, and became pastor of St. Martin of Tours, an old German parish fallen on hard times. He revived the place and did so with great success.

Later, on a trip to Europe, he decided that he owed Our Lady thanks and went to Chartres and found the little chapel, but the statue was gone. He asked the guard where they had moved it. "There was never any statue there and I've been here all my life." Father Robertson was much moved by that. Now his piety toward Our Lady was not only belief but experience as well.

Father Arnold was here some years ago. He was a cab driver in Milwaukee, was very short, very stout, and very German! He was accepted by a Benedictine abbey down south and on his way there stopped over here. The monks went to work on him and convinced him to stay here and join us, which he did. "Biggest mistake of my life," he used to say later, but you have to understand that Father Arnold was a character. He was quite given to ironic complaints and spoutings of no particular significance and little to do with reality.

He was ahead of me in the line one morning, waiting to speak with Dom James in the grand parlor after Prime. That was where you could see the abbot for permissions or other brief matters. Father Arnold asked the abbot if he could get a couple of packets of Morning Glory seeds. Spring was bursting out all over and Father Arnold loved flowers. He wanted these for some shrine. Dom James said, "No." Father Arnold got hot and said, "The brothers just bought a six-thousand-dollar tractor and I can't spend ten cents for a packet of seeds?" Dom James said, "They've gone up. They're twenty-five cents now." Father Arnold walked away fuming.

He used to work with Mass intentions and through the correspondence had lots of friends with whom he would stay in touch. So, when he would write to them he would tell them how hard it was to be a monk, ". . . couldn't even get a packet of seeds." They would take the hint and send him all kinds of seeds, more than he could plant. Of course, all involved knew what would happen.

So, is piety getting exceptional favors and visions? Is monastic life just a series of petty behaviors and unreasonable demands? Neither.

Yesterday was the anniversary of the Battle of Lepanto on October 7, 1571, the last great naval battle under oars. The Turks threatened the West, and Europe was in a panic over being overcome like Africa. Pius V was able to rally a fleet under Don Juan of Austria with Spain and Venice supporting him. Two hundred and six galleys were involved from the West with ninety thousand men. The Turks had 220 galleys, fifty smaller vessels, 120,000 soldiers and rowers, the latter Christian captives. The Christians' rowers were Moslem captives, prisoners, and hired recruits. Twelve thousand Christians were released by the victory, nine thousand were killed, thirty thousand Turks lost. Though the battle was a victory, Cyprus was lost anyway—the point at issue. But Moslem control of the Mediterranean was over. Pius V had called the Roman populace to the Rosary and in thanks instituted the feast of Our Lady of Victory. The next pope changed it to Our Lady of the Rosary, as we still have it.

So, is the faith a matter of war and bloodshed blessed by Our Lady? Not quite. There is darkness and light in every aspect of the human. Our Lady is indeed a tender Mother. Monastic life is a beautiful service and a glory of the Church. The Church is the Church of God and a Church of saints and sinners, high and low, facing life as they can.

If you would truly live, you need a vision, a vision that sees God in the human scene, in the Church and out of it, in darkness and light, in good and evil. They are always mixed in the world we know.

The twelve that Jesus picked were human. Of the twelve, all but one deserted him in his final hour. One denied him—the head of the group. One betrayed him and later hung himself. That motley group is the foundation of the church. Our Lady is their queen and ours. Today we consecrate anew this house and everyone in it to her, Our Lady of Gethsemani Abbey.

Amen.

DEATH AND BEYOND

A LOVELY FLOWER UNFOLDING

John 15:9-17

How did the disciples deal with the ascension of Christ? "Rejoice" characterized their first response, yet it surely was not long before a reaction set in and they were filled with sadness, softened only by the promise of the Spirit for an orphaned people.

One assumes they gathered—we know they did—and yet, during the first days after his rising, they must have done the same, if not in the Upper Room, then in casual pairs or clusters to do what anyone would do, what you and I would do. They talked. They shared memories, repeated what he had said, where he went, what he did. They must have gone back over the three years and lingered long over the final ending and the amazing resurrection.

Oral history. The first beginnings of the Gospels. Told and retold, lingered with. It would only be later that the final summary would be put down in written form, all in some way under the Spirit.

One wonders, too, if in those first days they broke bread and drank the cup. We do not know. Were there other appearances we do not know of, perhaps to encourage or to cheer? Were they aware of the full nature of the eucharistic meal? One thing is certain, they pondered and they prayed.

It turns out how like them we are, and how like us they were. For we gather, too, in small groups, in formal ones and in very casual ones, and do what they did. We remember. We tell familiar stories once again, what he said and what he did. We pray.

We do as they did. We break the bread of love and drink the cup of salvation. This has been going on for two thousand years.

There is still no end to the pondering, the reflecting, the commentary. We try, as they tried, to deal with it all, absorb it, enter into it, and be ever made new in it.

We call the whole business liturgy. They perhaps did not, but what was going on was the same. That is why we look on the New Testament as much a liturgical text as anything. It is the libretto, the script for the drama.

Though it is scarcely possible that they could have caught the full impact of what they were doing any more than we do, they must also have had the same subtle grasp that it was not mere gathering, mere talk, mere memory and recollection, the retelling of a familiar story in a setting of prayer.

Jesus lives in the gathering as he lives in the Word, as he lives in the sacrificial meal. That we experience his presence in every such encounter is in some way no historical recollection, no memorial day, but both that and fundamentally more. We relive the original, or better, are present.

This could only unfold in time in the Spirit, the original unfolding of some lovely flower slowly opening to reveal glorious hidden beauty. In the beginning they must have had some sense of that, even if poorly defined and inarticulate. The coming of the Spirit would enlighten and guide all.

Time is also timeless. There is a dimension to our experience of Christ which is not hampered or limited by time. We enter into another reality in which the past is truly present and the present truly past. Such insight is not so much the fruit of exceptional reasoning, as it is a matter of the heart where love reveals what the mind tries to express.

Time is such a frail, fragile entity, so mysterious. A man picks up a stone on the road to the hill and tells me it is probably two million years old! We are immersed in an eternity that we are part of, alive in. Our whole experience of the Christian mystery is revealed in the passing of each year of our lives, a story told over and over, entered into ever more deeply and fully.

Just as the original story involved ordinary people doing ordinary things each day of their lives, and yet caught up in something quite beyond the obvious, so we ordinary people doing ordinary things day after day walk in a timeless eternity that we will know fully when we enter into it wholly, which we will.

So we gather as they did. We tell it over again as they did. In the mystery of grace, of sacrament, or word heard, we not merely touch the eternal Christ, but we hear him, love him, and are embraced by him.

It is not a double life, it is a full one. We are not merely mortal, we are immortal, and we live both mortal and immortal lives every moment we are on earth.

As Christ left the earth for the life to come, so do we, sooner or later. We do so with the prayer in him and with him that all may know that eternal life made ours to come in Jesus Christ the Lord.

Amen.

O DEATH, WHERE IS THY STING

Mark 5:21-43

When I was living as a hermit in New Guinea, a young man would come by for a visit and chat for a while. Eventually, he would get to the point and slip me a dollar bill. "I'd like to see my son. You fix it so I can." Seeing that I was living alone on a hill by the sea, rising at night to pray, offering Mass and praying during the day, visiting the little missionary graveyard out back, he knew that I must see the dead and talk to them. It was obvious. I would tell him, "I don't see the dead." He would look at me and tell me, "You lie."

In times past they did see their dead, especially the young, for the death of the young devastated them. The death of the old they could manage, but the loss of his young son and not communing with him was overwhelming. I was tempted to tell them how their ancestors went into seclusion for a month, alone, and fasted. They would go into some semipsychotic state, hallucinate, and talk with their lost one. After a month they would emerge healed and at peace. But I did not tell him this for fear that they had lost the art they once had.

The death of the old is a mystery we can come to terms with in faith. We reckon its inevitability and somehow come to be reconciled with it, certain in terms of one's faith. It is rather the dead of the young that grieves us. Arbitrary death it seems to be. Haphazard. Needless. Cruel. If we can deal with the death of the elderly, we are much at a loss to cope with it in a child, a young man, a young woman.

One is reminded of the Holstein-Friesian cattle we had years ago up on the hill. Come spring they would have calves and, after some time, the calves would be taken from them and brought over on this side of the highway to the calf barn. Then on a moonlit night the cows would cry all night for the loss. There is surely no sadder sound than that of cows calling for their young. Even for dumb animals, the loss of young ones is a terrible loss indeed.

So it is the arbitrary aspect of the death of the young that Jesus faces up to in his miracles of raising the dead.

"*Talitha, kumi!* Young girl, I bid you rise!"

To the young son of the widow of Naim, "Young man, arise!"

To Lazarus, his friend and peer, "Lazarus, come forth!"

Death is one thing, the death of the young, another. "Old soldiers never die," intoned the aged General MacArthur at his retirement. "Yes," youth retorted, "but young ones do."

So, when Jesus confronts the last enemy, it is the enemy at its worst, in the young. It is more than death that he overcomes. It is the prodigal death which has moved forward from the inevitable death of the old to the arbitrary death of the young.

It does not make sense to cavil about Christ's miracles over death by saying, "What good are they? They died later on anyway: the little girl, the widow's son, Lazarus, and no doubt others."

Not true. They did not die. Not really. The death of a Christian is a transition, a passage through a door. It is leaving the womb of this life to be born to eternal life. There is no death for a person of faith.

That faith is not genuine unless there be death to sin by the rejection of evil and the acceptance of mercy. We are born in sin as the Pharisees said, so who are we to instruct others? Who are we? We are sinners, sinners whose sins are forgiven in the mercy of God. That is what a Christian is. The Christian will never die, whether death comes early or late, suddenly or gently. Christ triumphed over death, even the arbitrary, whimsical, haphazard death of the young.

We cannot say of Lazarus, "What good the raising since later on he would die anyway." No, he wouldn't. He would be born to eternal life. So will we all.

The tragedy of Jesus is not merely the tragedy of death, but death when you are young. The Virgin Mary, the mother of Jesus, did not die. It is not correct so to speak of her. As the *Catechism* has it:

> When the course of her earthly life was finished, she was taken up body and soul into heavenly glory and exalted by the Lord. (No. 966)

That was so because she was not involved in the Original Sin that brought death into the world. Her assumption anticipates our own resurrection on the last day.

Jesus, the sinless son of the living God, became sin for our sake and suffered the most tragic death when still a young man. Because he identified with us sinners, he submitted to death in order to overcome death.

His raising Lazarus was to express in anticipation his victory over death. The miracle of Lazarus became an expression of the basic thrust of Christ's life, death, and rising: the conquest of sin and death. Our engagement in all this is basic. The mystery of our life and death and rising is played out on the altar, in the Mass. Live.

Amen.

OUR NAMES ARE WRITTEN IN HEAVEN

Mark 12:38-44

If your nephew is visiting and you are pressed for something to talk about, I suggest Abraham Lincoln's birthplace. It is not far down the road and there is no charge. It is an interesting combination of great poverty and sheer elegance, a log cabin of the most primitive sort as the centerpiece to a massive, classic temple. Ancient Europe and backwoods Kentucky.

Probably the Eternal Dwelling Place is in mind, rather than the White House. One must take care in extolling the White House. After all, the Trumans had to move out lest the place fall down around them, so wretched was its condition. When Eleanor Roosevelt showed Mrs. Truman and daughter Margaret the place they were moving into, she casually remarked that there were rats in the White House. Rodents, that is.

The temple over the log cabin had something more in mind, the Eternal Home to come where, hopefully, we will all meet. If there is a President for whom this could be said, it is surely the name Lincoln that comes to mind.

The pathos of the Vietnam Memorial in Frankfort, overlooking our state capitol, is the names traced out in white granite, in calendar order, so arranged that the shadow of the huge sundial arm caresses your name on the day you died.

Perhaps it is better to say, on the day of your birth, for death is a passage to a new eternal life. That a body as far removed from us as the sun should figure in a relationship with a person's history is surely some attempt to see heavenly involvement with our life and our death. Our names are written in heaven and that a heavenly body like the sun should read them and note them on a day a person died is a gesture of some significance, a vehicle of deeper meaning. Our names are written in heaven. There is a place for us, and our names are known there.

My first encounter with death as a priest was with a young man burned in a grass fire while the men in his village were hunting pigs. They surrounded the pigs with fire and then speared them when they would dart free. He got caught in a wind change and all his skin was burned from his body except for his face. He was past pain because his nerves were burned away. I baptized him and anointed him. "Will you do me a favor?" I asked him. "You will be in heaven before the sun goes down. Will you mention my name when you get there? Your village? Your people?" "Sure," he said. So my name is not only written in heaven, it has been heard there!

The house we have here, be it ever so grand, be it ever so poverty-stricken, is at best a poor symbol of the house that awaits us in the Kingdom.

That our name may be wholly unknown here, or widely known, maybe ascribed to a university, a hospital, a town, or even a city, is nothing, indeed less than nothing when held up against our name being written in heaven. In Hebrew talk your name is you. Hence, do not take his name in vain. "Hallowed be thy name." "The name above all names." To be named on earth helps us to believe we are named in heaven. That is, we are to live there.

People who live in mansions have no guarantee of a heavenly one if there is no love in the house. A shanty by the tracks can speak as well of beauty to come when a loving heart is hidden in the poverty.

Our own departure to heaven as monks without benefit of as much as a wooden box is no doubt as comfortable as for the one buried in a bronze casket lined in satin with a mattress after a decent session of viewing and a final sealing in a cement vault impervious to ground water.

Let no one abuse you for your poverty. Be proud to give what you have and give it gladly. How many would be and wanna-be saints does it take to make one? How many singers to create a real voice? How many artists, dancers, actors, writers to bring a real one to birth? Thousands, thousands, no doubt. Yet, those thousands are necessary, are a seedbed for the ultimate gift.

It all matters and matters very much. None of it is trifling or of small account. One day the accumulated wealth breaks forth, the birth of an extraordinary gift of God, a response of many giving all to God, all their trifles, their pennies. Praise God.

Amen.

REHEARSAL FOR REALITY

Luke 2:16-21

I had a priest friend, an outgoing, hearty, friendly bear of a man. He taught. Every Christmas break he would serve as a chaplain on some cruise ship to the Caribbean. Travel companies and tourists loved him. He took a bit of drubbing from his brothers over the particular style of his ministry, but he would hold his ground, said he did a lot of good.

On one trip he learned that a Jewish couple was celebrating their silver wedding anniversary, so he got out his Hebrew Scripture and learned the blessing by heart, in Hebrew. Of course, the couple was deeply moved at the little ceremony. Who wouldn't be? In the original Hebrew.

> May the Lord bless you. May the Lord let his face shine on
> you and bring you peace.

Even in English it is very beautiful.

I cannot do it for you in Hebrew, but I do it. It is for your jubilee, New Year's Day. The end of one year, the start of another. The one we will never see again, the other we have never seen before. How many times for you? Past? Years to come?

It is multifaceted, multilayered, his feast, the Octave of Christmas. End of the old year. Start of the new. It's the circumcision, a Jewish rite. It's a Christmas feast. It's a secular one. As so many cards say, "Season's Greetings." "Health and Happiness for the New Year."

For our part, we can be very explicit, out loud: for God, for Jesus, for Mary, for Joseph, for the Old Law and the New. For the chosen and those grafted onto the chosen. A new year.

Father Paschal was here last year. And Brother Giles. And Brother Joseph. They are now what they were born for, where they were destined to be when God created them.

It is a wonderful thing to love life, and yet in loving know that it is a rehearsal for the real thing to come. A dress rehearsal, indeed, the final rehearsal, for the real thing is tomorrow night.

People say you cannot live like that, one foot here, one there, today with an eye on tomorrow. Yes, you can. You put your heart into it today because it colors and qualifies your tomorrow.

You rob this life of its inner meaning when you rob it of its eternal significance. Then you read into it what is not there. Our immortality is not negotiable. The desires are there and the desires are for union with God forever. To dismiss your immortality means you must seek to satisfy eternal desires with what is temporal, and then in one stroke frustrate both worlds.

"The Lord's face shining on you" means the eternal dimension is part of your reality. His light embraces the beauty of this world because it reads this world in terms of the next. Then everything is more than it is because faith reveals the scope of the human scene. Any human scene. Every human scene.

Not just silver weddings, not just Christmas, not just health and happiness, but the whole of it: darkness and light, sickness and health, suffering and death, the whole package.

> May the Lord bless you and keep you.
> May his light shine upon you.

Amen.